The Circuit

The Circuit

stories from the life
of a migrant child

Francisco Jiménez

Houghton Mifflin Company
Boston

Previously published in paperback by the University of New Mexico Press
The following stories have been previously published:
"The Circuit" in *The Arizona Quarterly*;
"Moving Still" in *California History*;
"Learning the Game" in *RiverSedge*.

Library of Congress Cataloging-in-Publication Data
Jiménez, Francisco, 1943–
The circuit: stories from the life of a migrant child
Francisco Jiménez.
p. cm.
ISBN 0-395-97902-1
1. Mexican Americans—California—Social life and customs—
Fiction. 2. Migrant agricultural laborers—California—Fiction.
3. Mexican American families—California—Fiction.
i. Title.
ps3560.i55c57 1997
813'ft.54—dc21   97-4844
cip

Manufactured in the United States of America
DOC 20 19 18
4500374304

To my parents and my seven sisters and brothers:
Avelina/*Rorra*
Evangelina/*Yerman*
María Luisa/*Licha*
Roberto/*Toto*
José Francisco/*Trampita*
Juan Manuel/*Torito*
and Rubén/*Carne Seca*

Contents

Acknowledgments, ix

Under the Wire, 1

Soledad, 8

Inside Out, 12

Miracle in Tent City, 22

El Angel de Oro, 36

Christmas Gift, 42

Death Forgiven, 47

Cotton Sack, 51

The Circuit, 61

Learning the Game, 70

To Have and to Hold, 80

Moving Still, 94

A Note from the Author, 112

Acknowledgments

There are many people who made this collection of short stories possible. I am indebted to my family whose lives are represented in this book. These stories are their stories as well as mine. These are also the stories of many migrant children of yesterday and today. I thank them all and ask their forgiveness for taking the liberty to write about them, knowing full well my limitations as a writer. Their courage, tenacity, and unwavering hope in the midst of adversity have been a constant inspiration to me.

Thanks to the many teachers and students who have written to me over the years about my work. Their particular interest in my story "The Circuit" and their encouragement to write more stories about my life have motivated me to continue writing.

I am grateful to my friends and colleagues who guided

me along the way with constructive criticism: Cedric Busette, *mi amigo del alma*; Kate Martin Fergueson; and Alma García. A special thanks to my immediate family for patiently listening to various drafts of the stories and offering valuable comments on them.

I would like to express my sincere gratitude to my teachers whose faith in my ability and whose guidance helped me break the migrant circuit.

I am thankful to Santa Clara University for giving me the time and encouragement to complete this book.

Finally, I am also indebted to my editor, Andrea Otañez, for her valuable suggestions for improvements and for her support.

The Circuit

Under the Wire

"*La frontera*" is a word I often heard when I was a child living in *El Rancho Blanco*, a small village nestled on barren, dry hills several miles north of Guadalajara, Mexico. I heard it for the first time back in the late 1940s when Papá and Mamá told me and Roberto, my older brother, that someday we would take a long trip north, cross *la frontera*, enter California, and leave our poverty behind.

I did not know exactly what California was either, but Papá's eyes sparkled whenever he talked about it with Mamá and his friends. "Once we cross *la frontera*, we'll make a good living in California," he would say, standing up straight and sticking out his chest.

Roberto, who is four years older than I, became excited every time Papá talked about the trip to California. He didn't like living in *El Rancho Blanco*, especially after visiting our older cousin, Fito, in Guadalajara.

Fito had left *El Rancho Blanco*. He was working in a tequila factory and living in a two-bedroom house that had electricity and a water well. He told Roberto that he, Fito, didn't have to get up at four in the morning anymore, like my brother, to milk the five cows by hand and carry the milk in a large aluminum can on horse for several miles to the nearest road, where a truck would transport it to town to sell. He didn't have to go to the river for water, sleep on dirt floors, or use candles for light.

From then on, about the only thing Roberto liked about living in *El Rancho Blanco* was hunting for chicken eggs and attending church on Sundays.

I liked looking for eggs and going to Mass too. But what I enjoyed most was listening to stories. In the evenings, after supper, Papá's brother, *tío* Mauricio, and his family came over to visit. We sat around a fire built with dry cow chips and told stories while shaking out grain from ears of corn.

On one such evening Papá made the announcement: We were going to make the long-awaited trip across *la frontera* to California. Days later we packed our belongings in a suitcase and took the bus to Guadalajara to catch the train. Papá bought tickets on a second-class train, *Ferrocarriles Nacionales de México*. I had never seen a train before. It looked like metal huts on wheels strung together. We climbed in and took our seats. I stood to look out the window. As the train started to move, it jerked and made a loud clattering sound, like hundreds of milk cans crashing. I got scared and lost my balance. Papá caught me and told me to sit. I swung my legs, following the rhythm of the train. Roberto sat across from me, next to Mamá. He had a big grin on his face.

We traveled for two days and nights. During the night, we didn't get much sleep. The wooden seats were hard, and the train made loud noises, blowing its whistle and grinding its brakes. At the first train stop I asked Papá, "Is this California?"

"No *mi'jo*, we're not there yet," he answered patiently. "We have many more hours to go."

Noting that Papá had closed his eyes, I turned to Roberto and asked, "What's California like?"

"I don't know," he answered, "but Fito told me that people there sweep money off the streets."

"Where did Fito get that idea?" Papá said, opening his eyes and laughing.

"From Cantinflas," Roberto said assuredly. "He said Cantinflas said it in a movie."

"Cantinflas was joking," Papá responded, chuckling. "But it's true that life is better there."

"I hope so," Mamá said. Then, putting her arm around Roberto, she added softly, "*Dios lo quiera.*"

The train slowed down. I looked out the window and saw we were entering another town. "Is this it?" I asked.

"*¡Otra vez la burra al trigo!*" Papá said, frowning and

rolling his eyes. "I'll tell you when we get there!"

"Be patient, Panchito," Mamá said, smiling. "We'll get there soon."

When the train stopped in Mexicali, Papá told us to get off. "We're almost there," he said, looking at me. We left the station. Papá carried our dark brown suitcase. We followed behind him until we reached a barbed wire fence. According to Papá, this was *la frontera*. He pointed out that across the gray wire barricade was California, that famous place I had heard so much about. On both sides of the fence were armed guards dressed in green uniforms. Papá called them *la migra*, and explained that we had to cross the fence to the other side without being seen by them.

Late that night, we walked for several miles away from town. Papá, who led the way, paused, looked all around to make sure no one could see us, and headed toward the fence. We walked along the wire wall until Papá spotted a small hole underneath the fence. Papá got on his knees and, with his hands, made the opening larger. We all crawled through like snakes. A few minutes later, we were picked up by a woman whom Papá had contacted in Mexicali. She had promised to pick us up in her car and drive us, for a fee, to a place where we would find work.

The woman drove all night, and at dawn we reached a tent labor camp on the outskirts of Guadalupe, a small town on the coast. She stopped the car by the side of a narrow road, near the camp.

"This is the place I told you about," she said wearily. "Here you'll find work picking strawberries."

Papá unloaded the suitcase from the trunk, took out his wallet, and paid the woman. "We have only seven dollars left," he said, biting his lower lip. After the woman drove away, we walked to the camp, following a dirt path lined on both sides by eucalyptus trees. Mamá held me by the hand very tightly. At the camp, Mamá and Papá were told that the foreman had left for the day.

We spent that night underneath the eucalyptus trees. We gathered leaves from the trees, which smelled like sweet gum, and piled them to lie on. Roberto and I slept between Papá and Mamá.

The following morning, I woke to the sound of a train whistle. For a split second I thought we were still on the train on our way to California. Spewing black smoke, it passed behind the camp, traveling much faster than the train we had taken from Guadalajara. As I followed it with my eyes, I heard a stranger's voice behind me. It was that of a woman who had stopped by to help. Her name was Lupe Gordillo; she was from the nearby camp. She brought us a few groceries and introduced us to the camp foreman, who spoke Spanish. He loaned us an army tent, which we pitched with his help. "You're lucky," he said. "This is the last tent we have."

"When can we start work?" Papá asked, rubbing his hands.

"In two weeks," the foreman answered.

"That can't be!" Papá exclaimed, shaking his head. "We were told we'd find work right away."

"I am sorry, the strawberries won't be ready to pick until then," the foreman responded, shrugging his shoulders and walking away.

After a long silence, Mamá said, "We'll manage, *viejo*. Once work starts, we'll be fine."

Roberto was quiet. He had a sad look in his eyes.

During the next two weeks, Mamá cooked outside on a makeshift stove using rocks and a *comal* Doña Lupe had given her. We ate wild *verdolagas* and rabbit and birds, which Papá hunted with a rifle he borrowed from a neighbor.

To pass the time, Roberto and I watched the trains go by behind the labor camp. We crawled underneath a barbed wire fence to get a closer look at them as they passed by several times a day.

Our favorite train came by every day at noon. It had a distinct whistle. We heard it coming from miles away. Roberto and I called it the Noon Train. Often, we would get there early and play on the railroad tracks while we waited for it. We ran straddling the rails or walked on them as fast as we could to see how far we could go without falling off. We also sat on the rails to feel them vibrate as the train approached. As days went by, we could recognize the conductor from afar. He slowed the train every time it went by and waved at us with his gray-and-white striped cap. We waved back.

One Sunday, Roberto and I crossed the fence earlier than usual to wait for the Noon Train. Roberto didn't feel like playing, so we sat on one of the rails, arms wrapped around our legs, foreheads on our knees. "I wonder where the train comes from," I said. "Do you know, Roberto?"

"I have been wondering too," he answered, slowly lifting his head. "I think it comes from California."

"California!" I exclaimed. "This is California!"

"I am not so sure," he said. "Remember what—"

The familiar Noon Train whistle interrupted him. We stepped off the rail and moved a few feet away from the tracks. The conductor slowed the train to a crawl, waved, and gently dropped a large brown bag in front of us as he went by. We picked it up and looked inside. It was full of oranges, apples, and candy.

"See, it does come from California!" Roberto exclaimed. We ran alongside the train, waving at the conductor. The train sped up and soon left us behind. We followed the rear of the train with our eyes until it got smaller and smaller and disappeared.

Soledad

That cold, early morning, Papá parked the *Carcachita*,
our old jalopy, at one end of the cotton field. He,
Mamá, and Roberto, my older brother, climbed out and
headed toward the other end, where the picking started.
As usual, they left me alone in the car to take care of
Trampita, my little brother, who was six months old. I
hated being left by myself with him while they went off
to pick cotton.

As they walked farther into the field, I climbed onto
the roof of the car, stood on tiptoe, and watched them
until I could no longer tell them apart from the other
pickers. Once I lost sight of them, I felt pain in my chest,
that same pain I always felt whenever they left Trampita
and me alone. Sobbing, I climbed into the car and wrapped
my arms around Trampita, who slept in the back seat. He
woke up crying and shivering from the cold. I covered

him with a small blanket and gave him his bottle of milk. He calmed down and went back to sleep.

After several long hours, I climbed onto the roof of the car again to see if Papá, Mamá, and Roberto were on their way back for lunch. I looked as far away as I could, without blinking, hoping to spot them. When I finally saw them, my heart started racing. I jumped off the car, fell to the ground, got up, and ran to meet them. I almost knocked Roberto off his feet when I jumped on him.

After checking on Trampita, Mamá and Papá spread a green army blanket on the ground behind the *Carcachita*, where we all sat to eat. Mamá reached into a large grocery bag and pulled out the tacos she had prepared for us at dawn that morning. Papá ate quickly because he did not want to lose time from work. Roberto and I ate slowly, trying to make time last a bit longer. Holding him in her left arm, Mamá nursed Trampita while she ate with her right hand. She then laid him on the back seat of the car, changed his diaper, and kissed him gently on his forehead as he closed his eyes and fell asleep. Papá got up, folded the blanket, and placed it back inside the trunk of the car. He then picked up his empty cotton sack and flipped it over his left shoulder. This was the signal for Roberto and Mamá that it was time to go back to work.

I climbed onto the roof of the *Carcachita* again and watched them disappear into the sea of cotton. My eyes began to cloud up. I climbed off the car and, leaning against the back tire, I sat and thought, "If I learn to pick cotton, Papá will let me go with him, Mamá, and Roberto, and I won't be left alone anymore!"

After checking on Trampita to make sure he was still asleep, I quietly walked over to the row nearest the car and picked cotton for the first time.

It was not as easy as I thought. I tried to pick with both hands, just like Roberto, but could only pick one cotton boll at a time. I held the cotton shells steady from underneath with my left hand while I picked the bolls with my right hand and piled them on the ground. The shells' sharp prongs scratched my hands like cat's claws and, sometimes, dug into the corner of my fingernails and made them bleed. I had trouble reaching the cotton bolls at the very top of the tall plants, so I leaned against the plants and pushed them over with my body until they touched the ground. I then stood on them while I stooped over and picked the cotton bolls. I had to step off to the side quickly because the plants sprang back like a bow, whipping me in the face if I did not move fast enough.

At the end of the day, I was tired and disappointed. I had not picked as much cotton as I had wanted to. The pile was only about two feet high. Then I remembered Papá saying that we got paid three cents a pound, so I mixed dirt clods with the cotton to make it weigh more.

At dusk, Papá, Mamá, and Roberto finally returned. I was about to tell them my surprise when Mamá interrupted me. "How is Trampita?" she asked, going straight to the car to check on him. When she opened the car door and saw him, she was angry. I had been so busy learning to pick cotton that I had forgotten all about him. Tired from crying, he had fallen asleep after soiling himself and dropping and breaking the bottle of milk. "I told you to take care of Trampita!" Mamá shouted.

"But look what I did," I said, proudly pointing to my pile of cotton.

Mamá glanced at the pile, shook her head in anger, and began cleaning Trampita. Papá looked at my cotton, grinned slightly, and asked Roberto to help him collect it. His grin quickly turned into a frown when he discovered the dirt clods. He separated them from the cotton, pointing them out one by one as he tossed them on the ground. "You should be ashamed of yourself. We could be fired for this," he said. "Besides, your job is to take care of Trampita. Is that clear?" he continued, placing both hands on his belt buckle.

"*Sí, Papá,*" I answered timidly. I was hurt and confused. Seeking comfort, I walked over to Roberto and whispered to him, "Someday, I will get to go pick cotton with you, Papá, and Mamá. Then I won't be left alone." Roberto put his arm around me and nodded his head.

Inside Out

"I remember being hit on the wrists with a twelve-inch ruler because I did not follow directions in class," Roberto answered in a mildly angry tone when I asked him about his first year of school. "But how could I?" he continued. "The teacher gave them in English."

"So what did you do?" I asked, rubbing my wrists.

"I always guessed what the teacher wanted me to do. And when she did not use the ruler on me, I knew I had guessed right," he responded. "Some of the kids made fun of me when I tried to say something in English and got it wrong," he went on. "I had to repeat first grade."

I wish I had not asked him, but he was the only one in the family, including Papá and Mamá, who had attended school. I walked away. I did not speak or understand English either, and I already felt anxious. Besides, I was excited about going to school for the first time that following

Monday. It was late January and we had just returned, a week before, from Corcoran, where my family picked cotton. We settled in Tent City, a labor camp owned by Sheehey Strawberry Farms located about ten miles east of Santa Maria.

On our first day of school, Roberto and I got up early. I dressed in a pair of overalls, which I hated because they had suspenders, and a flannel checked shirt, which Mamá had bought at the Goodwill store. As I put on my cap, Roberto reminded me that it was bad manners to wear a hat indoors. I thought of leaving it at home so that I would not make the mistake of forgetting to take it off in class, but I decided to wear it. Papá always wore a cap, and I did not feel completely dressed for school without it.

On our way out to catch the school bus, Roberto and I said good-bye to Mamá. Papá had already left to look for work, either topping carrots or thinning lettuce. Mamá stayed home to take care of Trampita, and to rest because she was expecting another baby.

When the school bus arrived, Roberto and I climbed in and sat together. I took the window seat and, on the way, watched endless rows of lettuce and cauliflower whiz by. The furrows that came up to the two-lane road looked like giant legs running alongside us. The bus made several stops to pick up kids and, with each stop, the noise inside got louder. Some kids were yelling at the top of their lungs. I did not know what they were saying. I was getting a headache. Roberto had his eyes closed and was frowning. I did not disturb him. I figured he was getting a headache too.

By the time we got to Main Street School, the bus was packed. The bus driver parked in front of the red brick building and opened the door. We all poured out. Roberto, who had attended the school the year before, accompanied me to the main office, where we met the principal, Mr. Sims, a tall, red-headed man with bushy eyebrows and hairy hands. He patiently listened to Roberto, who, using the little English he knew, managed to enroll me in the first grade.

Mr. Sims walked me to my classroom. I liked it as soon as I saw it because, unlike our tent, it had wooden floors, electric lights, and heat. It felt cozy. He introduced me to my teacher, Miss Scalapino, who smiled, repeating my name, "Francisco." It was the only word I understood the whole time she and the principal talked. They repeated it each time they glanced at me. After he left, she showed me to my desk, which was at the end of the row of desks closest to the windows. There were no other kids in the room yet.

I sat at my desk and ran my hand over its wooden top. It was full of scratches and dark, almost black, ink spots. I opened the top, and inside were a book, a box of crayons, a yellow ruler, a thick pencil, and a pair of scissors. To my left, under the windows, was a dark wooden counter the length of the room. On top of it, right next to my desk, was a caterpillar in a large jar. It looked just like the ones I had seen in the fields. It was yellowish green with black bands and it moved very slowly, without making any sound.

I was about to put my hand in the jar to touch the caterpillar when the bell rang. All the kids lined up outside the classroom door and then walked in quietly and took their seats. Some of them looked at me and giggled. Embarrassed and nervous, I looked at the caterpillar in the jar. I did this every time someone looked at me.

Miss Scalapino started speaking to the class and I did not understand a word she was saying. The more she spoke, the more anxious I became. By the end of the day, I was very tired of hearing Miss Scalapino talk because the sounds made no sense to me. I thought that perhaps by paying close attention, I would begin to understand, but I did not. I only got a headache, and that night, when I went to bed, I heard her voice in my head.

For days I got headaches from trying to listen, until I learned a way out. When my head began to hurt, I let my mind wander. Sometimes I imagined myself flying out of the classroom and over the fields where Papá worked and landing next to him and surprising him. But when I daydreamed, I continued to look at the teacher and pretend I was paying attention because Papá told me it was disrespectful not to pay attention, especially to grownups.

It was easier when Miss Scalapino read to the class from a book with illustrations because I made up my own stories, in Spanish, based on the pictures. She held the book with both hands above her head and walked around the classroom to make sure everyone got a chance to see the pictures, most of which were of animals. I enjoyed looking at them and making up stories, but I wished I understood what she was reading.

In time I learned some of my classmates' names. The one I heard the most and therefore learned first was Curtis. Curtis was the biggest, strongest, and most popular kid in the class. Everyone wanted to be his friend and to play with him. He was always chosen captain when the kids formed teams. Since I was the smallest kid in the class and did not know English, I was chosen last.

I preferred to hang around Arthur, one of the boys who knew a little Spanish. During recess, he and I played on the swings and I pretended to be a Mexican movie star, like Jorge Negrete or Pedro Infante, riding a horse and singing the *corridos* we often heard on the car radio. I sang them to Arthur as we swung back and forth, going as high as we could.

But when I spoke to Arthur in Spanish and Miss Scalapino heard me, she said *"No!"* with body and soul. Her head turned left and right a hundred times a second, and her index finger moved from side to side as fast as a windshield wiper on a rainy day. "English, English," she repeated. Arthur avoided me whenever she was around.

Often during recess I stayed with the caterpillar. Sometimes it was hard to spot him because he blended in with the green leaves and twigs. Every day I brought him leaves from the pepper and cypress trees that grew on the playground.

Just in front of the caterpillar, lying on top of the cabinet, was a picture book of caterpillars and butterflies. I went through it, page by page, studying all the pictures and running my fingers lightly over the caterpillars and the bright wings of the butterflies and the many patterns on them. I knew caterpillars turned into butterflies because Roberto had told me, but I wanted to know more. I was sure information was in the words written underneath each picture in large black letters. I tried to figure them out by looking at the pictures. I did this so many times that I could close my eyes and see the words, but I could not understand what they meant.

My favorite time in school was when we did art, which was every afternoon, after the teacher had read to us. Since I did not understand Miss Scalapino when she explained the art lessons, she let me do whatever I wanted. I drew all kinds of animals but mostly birds and butterflies. I sketched them in pencil and then colored them using every color in my crayon box. Miss Scalapino even tacked one of my drawings up on the board for everyone to see. After a couple of weeks it disappeared, and I did not know how to ask where it had gone.

One cold Thursday morning, during recess, I was the

only kid on the playground without a jacket. Mr. Sims must have noticed I was shivering because that afternoon, after school, he took me to his office and pulled out a green jacket from a large cardboard box that was full of used clothes and toys. He handed it to me and gestured for me to try it on. It smelled like graham crackers. I put it on, but it was too big, so he rolled up the sleeves about two inches to make it fit. I took it home and showed it off to my parents. They smiled. I liked it because it was green and it hid my suspenders.

The next day I was on the playground wearing my new jacket and waiting for the first bell to ring when I saw Curtis coming at me like an angry bull. Aiming his head directly at me, and pulling his arms straight back with his hands clenched, he stomped up to me and started yelling. I did not understand him, but I knew it had something to do with the jacket because he began to pull on it, trying to take it off me. The next thing I knew he and I were on the ground wrestling. Kids circled us. I could hear them yelling Curtis's name and something else. I knew I had no chance, but I stubbornly held on to my jacket. He pulled on one of the sleeves so hard that it ripped at the shoulder. He pulled on the right pocket and it ripped. Then Miss Scalapino's face appeared above. She pushed Curtis off of me and grabbed me by the back of the collar and picked me up off the ground. It took all the power I had not to cry.

On the way to the classroom Arthur told me that Curtis

claimed the jacket was his, that he had lost it at the beginning of the year. He also said that the teacher told Curtis and me that we were being punished. We had to sit on the bench during recess for the rest of the week. I did not see the jacket again. Curtis got it but I never saw him wear it.

For the rest of the day, I could not even pretend I was paying attention to Miss Scalapino; I was so embarrassed. I laid my head on top of my desk and closed my eyes. I kept thinking about what had happened that morning. I wanted to fall asleep and wake up to find it was only a dream. The teacher called my name but I did not answer. I heard her walk up to me. I did not know what to expect. She gently shook me by the shoulders. Again, I did not respond. Miss Scalapino must have thought I was asleep because she left me alone, even when it was time for recess and everyone left the room.

Once the room was quiet, I slowly opened my eyes. I had had them closed for so long that the sunlight coming through the windows blinded me. I rubbed my eyes with the back of my hands and then looked to my left at the jar. I looked for the caterpillar but could not see it. Thinking it might be hidden, I put my hand in the jar and lightly stirred the leaves. To my surprise, the caterpillar had spun itself into a cocoon and had attached itself to a small twig. It looked like a tiny cotton bulb, just like Roberto had said it would. I gently stroked it with my index finger, picturing it asleep and peaceful.

At the end of the school day, Miss Scalapino gave me a note to take home to my parents. Papá and Mamá did not know how to read, but they did not have to. As soon as they saw my swollen upper lip and the scratches on my left cheek, they knew what the note said. When I told them what happened, they were very upset but relieved that I did not disrespect the teacher.

For the next several days, going to school and facing Miss Scalapino was harder than ever. However, I slowly began to get over what happened that Friday. Once I got used to the routine in school and I picked up some English words, I felt more comfortable in class.

On Wednesday, May 23, a few days before the end of the school year, Miss Scalapino took me by surprise. After we were all sitting down and she had taken roll, she called for everyone's attention. I did not understand what she said, but I heard her say my name as she held up a blue ribbon. She then picked up my drawing of the butterfly that had disappeared weeks before and held it up for everyone to see. She walked up to me and handed me the drawing and the silk blue ribbon that had the number one printed on it in gold. I knew then I had received first prize for my drawing. I was so proud I felt like bursting out of my skin. My classmates, including Curtis, stretched their necks to see the ribbon.

That afternoon, during our free period, I went over to check on the caterpillar. I turned the jar around, trying to see the cocoon. It was beginning to crack open. I excitedly cried out, "Look, look," pointing to it. The whole class, like a swarm of bees, rushed over to the counter. Miss Scalapino took the jar and placed it on top of a desk in the middle of the classroom so everyone could see it. For the next several minutes we all stood there watching the butterfly emerge from its cocoon, in slow motion.

At the end of the day, just before the last bell, Miss Scalapino picked up the jar and took the class outside to the playground. She placed the jar on the ground and we all circled around her. I had a hard time seeing over the other kids, so Miss Scalapino called me and motioned for me to open the jar. I broke through the circle, knelt on the ground, and unscrewed the top. Like magic, the butterfly flew into the air, fluttering its wings up and down.

After school I waited in line for my bus in front of the playground. I proudly carried the blue ribbon in my right hand and the drawing in the other. Arthur and Curtis came up and stood behind me to wait for their bus. Curtis motioned for me to show him the drawing again. I held it up so he could see it.

"He really likes it, Francisco," Arthur said to me in Spanish.

"*¿Cómo se dice 'es tuyo' en inglés?*" I asked.

"It's yours," answered Arthur.

"It's yours," I repeated, handing the drawing to Curtis.

Miracle in Tent City

We called it Tent City. Everybody called it Tent City, although it was neither a city nor a town. It was a farm worker labor camp owned by Sheehey Strawberry Farms.

Tent City had no address; it was simply known as rural Santa Maria. It was on Main Street, about ten miles east of the center of town. Half a mile east of it were hundreds of acres of strawberries cultivated by Japanese sharecroppers and harvested by people from the camp. Behind Tent City was dry wilderness, and a mile north of it was the city dump. Many of the residents in the camp were single men, most of whom, like us, had crossed the border illegally. There were a few single women and a few families, all Mexican.

Mamá was already expecting when we moved to Tent City from Corcoran at the end of January, after the cotton season was over. By May, when the strawberry harvest started, she was only a few weeks away from giving birth, so she did not join Papá in the fields picking strawberries for Ito. She could not bend over, and picking on her knees was too hard on her.

To make ends meet, Mamá cooked for twenty farm workers who lived in Tent City. She made their lunches and had supper ready for them when they returned from picking strawberries at the end of the day. She would get up at four o'clock every morning, seven days a week, to make the tortillas for both meals. On weekends and all during the summer, Roberto and I helped her. Once Papá left for work, Roberto rolled the tacos while I wrapped them in wax paper and put them in lunch bags. At eleven-thirty, Roberto carried the twenty lunches in a box and delivered them, on foot, to the workers, who were given half an hour for lunch. When he returned, he and I washed dishes in a large aluminum tub. We then took care of our younger brother, Trampita, while Mamá took a nap. Around three o'clock she would start cooking dinner, which was served from six to seven. After supper, Roberto and I again cleaned the pots and washed dishes while Mamá fed Trampita. On Saturdays, she did all of the grocery shopping for the week. Because we did not have an icebox, Papá made one. Every three days, he went into town to buy a large block of ice, which he wrapped in burlap and placed inside a hole he dug in the ground by the entrance to our tent. The hole was twice as large as the block of ice, leaving room on all four sides and on top for things to be kept cold.

Even though Mamá was always tired from all the work she did, she made sure everything was ready for the new baby. She asked Papá to seal the base of the tent by piling extra dirt, about six inches high, all around it outside so that animals, especially snakes, could not crawl underneath during the night. When Papá had finished, Mamá pleaded with him to build a floor. He agreed, and every evening after he came home from work, he sent Roberto and me to the city dump to look for discarded lumber to build a floor inside our tent.

Our trip to the dump was always an adventure. We waited until dusk, after the dump caretaker left, before raiding for treasures because we had no money to buy them. When he went home in the evenings, the caretaker locked the more valuable items, such as used clothing, car parts, and broken lamps, in a makeshift shed. The larger pieces — mattresses, box springs, broken pieces of furniture — he left outside, leaning against the storehouse. Besides lumber, I collected books, hoping to read them once I learned how. My favorites were those with pictures.

Late one evening, thinking the caretaker had left, Roberto and I sneaked into the dump. The dump keeper, who had hidden behind one of the mounds of rubbish, took us by surprise. He chased us, yelling and cursing in broken Spanish. We were scared and went home empty-handed that night, but we went back several more times until we got enough lumber to complete Mamá's floor. We also found pieces of linoleum and laid them over the wood to cover the holes and slivers. The different shapes and colors made the floor look like a quilt.

On one of our trips we found a large wooden box that became the crib for the new baby. Mamá took an old green army blanket, tore it in half, and lined the box with it. She made a little pillow with stuffing from an old mattress and cloth from a white flour sack.

Mamá also made sure the entrance to our tent was always closed to keep out the smoke and odor from the camp's garbage dump, located directly in front of our tent, twenty yards away. It was a large rectangular hole dug in the dirt, about six feet long by four feet wide and three feet deep. On windy days, the foul smell of the city dump competed with the stench of the Tent City dump. The older neighborhood kids killed snakes and threw them in the garbage hole when it was burning and watched them sizzle and squirm. I could not figure out why they twisted and turned in the fire after they were dead. It was as though the fire brought them back to life. Once Trampita got too close to the garbage hole and fell in. Roberto pulled him out. Luckily it was not burning. From then on, Papá did not let us play near it.

When the baby was finally born, Roberto, Trampita, and I were excited to see him, especially because we had worked so hard to get things ready for him. Papá and Mamá named him Juan Manuel, but we all called him Torito, or little bull, because he weighed ten pounds at birth. He had a chubby, round face and curly brown hair. I thought the nickname Torito fitted him because he had a strong grip. I would put two of my fingers in his tiny hand, and when I tried pulling away, he would not let go and would kick with both feet. When Mamá nursed him, he closed his eyes and played with her hair. Whenever I changed his diaper, I made him laugh by tickling his stomach.

I liked playing with Torito because he was always cheerful, and because he helped me forget about the report card I got in early June, a few days before he was born. Miss Scalapino, my first-grade teacher, said I had to repeat her class because I did not know English.

About two months after he was born, Torito got sick. I knew there was something wrong with him when he cried off and on all during the night. The next morning when I tickled him he did not even smile. He looked pale. Mamá, who had not slept much that night either, touched his forehead.

"I think Torito has a fever," she said, a bit flustered. "Please look after him while Roberto and I prepare the lunches."

I touched my forehead and then Torito's to see if I could tell the difference. His felt a lot hotter. I then changed his soiled diaper. It smelled terrible. That afternoon, Mamá had to change him often. His thighs and bottom got as red as the back of Papá's sunburned neck. By the afternoon of the following day, the aluminum tub was almost filled with soiled diapers. To rinse them, I got water in a bucket from the faucet, which was located a few feet from the outhouse in the middle of the camp. Luckily, I did not have to wait in line too long. Only one woman, with two buckets, was ahead of me. Once she finished, I filled my bucket and carried it back to our tent. I poured the water in the diaper tub and rinsed the diapers with my right hand while I held my nose with my left. Mamá then heated water in a pot, poured it into another tub, washed the diapers on a washboard, and hung them up to dry outside on a clothesline Papá made.

Mamá bathed Torito in cold water several times a day, trying to bring his fever down, but it did not do any good. In the evenings we prayed for him in front of a faded picture of the *Virgen de Guadalupe*, which was tied with string to the canvas wall above the mattress.

One night as we were praying, Torito got worse. He stiffened and clenched his arms and legs, and his eyes rolled back. Saliva dribbled from both sides of his mouth. His lips turned purple. He stopped breathing. Thinking he was dead, I started crying hysterically. Roberto and Mamá did too. Trampita got scared and began to whimper. Papá tried to pry open Torito's mouth but could not. His jaws were locked. Mamá picked him up from the box and held him tightly against her chest. "Please God, don't take him away, please," Mamá repeated over and over again. Torito slowly began to breathe. His arms and legs relaxed. I could see the brown color of his eyes again. We all sighed with relief, wiping our tears with the backs of our hands and crying and laughing at the same time.

No one slept well that night. Torito woke up crying several times. The next morning, Mamá's eyes were puffy and red. She took a lot longer than usual to make the tortillas and the lunches. After Papá left for work, and Roberto and I washed the dishes, Mamá kept her eyes glued on Torito. She gave him water and tried to nurse him, but she was not producing enough milk, so she prepared him a bottle. By the afternoon, she could hardly keep her head up. Roberto and I convinced her to take a nap while we took care of Torito.

Mamá had trouble falling asleep. When she finally did, Torito started crying. She jumped out of bed, picked him up in her arms, and rocked him, trying to calm him. Once he quieted down, she asked Roberto and me to clean the beans to cook for supper. "That's all we'll have tonight," she said apologetically, "*frijoles de la olla*. I hope the boarders won't mind."

"They won't," I responded, placing the bean pot on the kerosene stove.

That evening, after supper, Mamá laid Torito on the mattress to change him. When she pulled the front of the soiled diaper off and saw blood, she screamed at Papá, "*Viejo*, he is getting worse! Look, there's blood in his stool!"

Papá rushed over and knelt on the mattress next to Torito, who started to moan. He felt Torito's forehead and stomach. "He still has a fever," Papá said pensively. "His stomach feels hard. Maybe it's something he ate. If he doesn't get better soon, we'll have to take him to the hospital."

"But we don't have any money," Mamá responded, sobbing and looking sadly at Torito.

"We'll borrow, or...something," Papá said, putting his right arm around Mamá's shoulder.

Papá was about to continue when Doña María, our next door neighbor, interrupted him. "Can I come in?" she asked, poking her head in the entrance to our tent.

Doña María was known in Tent City as *la curandera* because she had a gift for curing people using different herbs and chants. She was tall and slender and always wore black dresses that matched the color of her straight, long hair. Her skin was ruddy and pockmarked, and her eyes were deep set and light green. Tied around her waist was a small, purple velvet bag that jingled when she walked.

"Come in," Papá answered.

"I've been hearing your baby cry," Doña María continued. "What's wrong with him?"

"We don't know," Mamá answered.

"Could it be the evil eye?" asked Doña María, holding the velvet bag in the palm of her left hand. "He is a very handsome child."

"*¿El mal de ojo?* No, I think it's his stomach. It's as hard as a rock. Feel it," Papá responded, bringing the kerosene lamp closer to Torito so she could get a better look at him.

Doña María gently rubbed Torito's stomach with her bony right hand. As soon as she pressed down on it, he groaned and started to cry. She turned him over on his stomach and with her left hand pulled up a fold of skin from his back and then released it. After doing this three times, she flipped him over on his back and asked Mamá to bring her three eggs. She cracked the eggs on his stomach and massaged him gently with them. "The eggs will draw out his sickness," she said confidently. Torito stopped crying. Mamá seemed relieved, but I was not. There was something about *la curandera* that made me nervous.

Moments after Doña María left, just as we were getting ready for bed, Torito started moaning. Then he suddenly stopped. There was dead silence. We all looked at each other and rushed to his side. He was as stiff as a board and had stopped breathing. His eyes were rolled back. Mamá started weeping. Like Roberto and Trampita, I cried too. I felt very scared. *Perhaps Doña María made him worse*, I thought.

Papá quickly picked up Torito, wrapped him in a blanket, and yelled, "*¡Vieja, vámonos al hospital!*" He and Mamá ran out and took off in the *Carcachita*. Roberto, Trampita, and I stood there, crying.

I thought I would never see Torito again. Frightened

and confused I walked outside. It was pitch dark and quiet. I went behind our tent, knelt down on rocky ground, and prayed for Torito for a very long time, until my parents returned.

As soon as I heard the *Carcachita*, I got up from my knees and ran to the front of the tent to meet them. When I saw Mamá and Papá without Torito, I panicked. "Is he dead?" I cried out.

"No, Panchito; calm down," Papá answered. "We left him at the hospital."

"Is he going... to die?" I stammered.

"No, he isn't," Mamá snapped. "God won't let him. You'll see," she added in a harsh tone. Her face was flushed and her dark eyes were full of tears. I was surprised and puzzled. Why would she be angry at me?

That night I had trouble sleeping, thinking about Torito. Mamá and Papá did not sleep either. I heard Mamá sobbing every time I woke up and saw Papá smoking one cigarette after another.

Early the next morning, Mamá said she was going to drive Papá to work. I thought it was strange because Papá always took the car to go pick strawberries. Besides, it was only five-thirty. Papá did not have to be at work until seven, and it only took a few minutes to get there. "I'll be right back," Mamá said, looking at Roberto and me. "Be sure to take care of Trampita."

I followed my parents to the car and as Mamá was about

to get in it, I asked, "Can we go see Torito when you get back?" Mamá closed the car door without answering and sped off. Roberto and I went back in the tent. We did not say a word to each other, but each of us knew what the other was thinking. We knelt side by side on the mattress, in front of the *Virgen de Guadalupe*, and prayed silently.

I was worried and irritated by the time Mamá returned. It was around eleven. "Where were you?" I asked angrily. "I want to go see Torito."

"Only if God wills it," she said sadly, putting her arms around Roberto and me.

"What do you mean?" I asked.

"Torito is very sick," she replied. "He has a rare disease that may be catching. That's why you can't see him."

"But you went to see him this morning, didn't you?" I responded, raising my voice. "That's why you took so long, right?"

"*Sí, mi'jo*," she answered, "but they won't let children in to see him. You can see him when he comes home."

"When is that?" Roberto and I asked at the same time.

"Soon, probably," she answered hesitantly.

I had a feeling Mamá was not telling us all she knew.

After preparing supper, Mamá went to pick up Papá from work. When they got home, Papá looked very upset and anxious. I waited for them to talk about Torito, but they did not say a word about him. And as soon as dinner was over, they left for the hospital. After Roberto and I cleaned the dishes, I went outside, behind our tent, and prayed on my knees again. But only for a little while. I hurried inside when I heard Doña María chanting next door.

When Papá and Mamá returned from the hospital, Mamá's arms were empty. Roberto and I looked at each other in disappointment. "Torito is a little better, but we can't bring him home until tomorrow," she said, teary-eyed and with a feigned smile. Then taking a deep breath, and looking at Roberto, Trampita, and me, she continued, "We have to pray to the *Santo Niño de Atocha* because —"

"Yes," Papá interrupted, taking out his wallet and pulling out a tattered holy card. "Your Mamá and I have made a promise to *el Santo Niño*." Then holding the card in the palm of his right hand and looking at it, he continued, "We'll pray to him every day, for a whole year, if Torito gets well."

Papá then took a pin from a small tin box where Mamá kept her sewing things and pinned the card to the canvas wall, above the mattress, next to the picture of the *Virgen de Guadalupe*.

On the holy card was a picture of the little Jesus of Atocha sitting on a high wooden chair. He wore sandals, a blue cloak, a short, brown cape, and a brimmed hat to match. In his right hand he carried a basket and in his left hand a wooden staff.

We all knelt in front of the *Santo Niño* to pray. Mamá always prayed to him whenever one of us got sick because she said the Holy Child Jesus took care of poor and sick people, especially children. The late hour and the repetition of the prayers made me sleepy.

That night I dreamed about the *Santo Niño de Atocha*. I was behind our tent, praying on my knees in front of the baby Jesus holy card. Suddenly the *Santo Niño* came alive. He stood up from his chair and floated in the air, carrying the basket. He glided to where I was and placed the basket at my feet and pointed to it. Out of the basket emerged hundreds of tiny white butterflies. They formed themselves into a pair of wings, lifting me and carrying me away over Tent City and setting me down next to my Torito, who lay in the middle of a lush-green alfalfa field. In the dream I awoke and looked at the prayer card. Torito was in it, sitting in the high chair, dressed as the *Santo Niño de Atocha*.

The next morning, when I told Mamá about my dream, she decided to make Torito an outfit, just like the one the *Santo Niño de Atocha* was wearing in the picture prayer card. Instead of taking a nap after she made the lunches, she started sewing a cloak using the fabric from one of her blue dresses. She finished it that evening, just in time to go get Torito from the hospital.

Later that night, when Mamá and Papá returned with Torito from the hospital, he was wearing the blue cloak Mamá had made him, but he did not look like the *Santo Niño* in the holy card. Torito was pale and skinny.

He moaned when I tickled him. "Mamá, is Torito still sick?" I asked.

"Yes, *mi'jo*," she responded, "that's why we have to keep on praying."

"But didn't the doctor take care of him?"

Mamá turned her back to me and did not respond. I looked at Papá, who was pacing up and down, wringing his hands. After a long moment of silence, he said, "Remember, we have to keep our promise and pray to *el Santo Niño* every day, for a whole year."

That night, and every night for an entire year, we all prayed to *el Santo Niño de Atocha* as we followed the crops from place to place. During that time, Mamá dressed Torito in the blue cloak and only took it off when it needed to be washed.

On August 17, the day we completed the promise to *el Santo Niño*, we all gathered around Torito, who sat on Mamá's lap. His chubby, rosy cheeks made him look like a cherub.

"I have something to tell you," Mamá said teary-eyed as she took off his cloak. "When we took Torito to the hospital, the doctor told us my son would die because we had waited too long to take him there. He said it would take a miracle for him to live. I didn't want to believe him," she continued, gaining strength as she talked. "But he was right. It took a miracle."

El Angel de Oro

For Miguel Antonio

It always rained a lot in Corcoran during the cotton season, but that year it rained more than usual. No sooner had we arrived from Fowler, where we had picked grapes, than it started to pour. Our cabin was one of several farm-worker shacks lined up in a row, behind which ran a small creek.

There was not a lot to do when it rained. We stayed indoors telling ghost stories we had heard from other migrant workers. We also played guessing games. When I got tired of listening to the same stories told many times before, I watched our neighbor's goldfish. From our window I could see into the next cabin, where a fishbowl sat on a small table. I spent hours glued to our window, watching the goldfish glide in slow motion, stirring the jade green plants with its delicate fins. Mamá enjoyed watching it too. She called it *el Angel de Oro*.

Papá passed most of his time worrying. He smoked one cigarette after another and complained about the rain because we could not pick the cotton when it was wet. "If this rain doesn't stop we'll have to leave and find work somewhere else," he repeated, pacing up and down the floor. Even the thought of rain gave him a headache. Luckily for me, I got to go to school the following week.

Monday morning, after getting Mamá's blessing, I headed for school, which was only about a mile from the cotton labor camp. I could see it from where we lived. On the way, I met Miguelito, who lived in the same labor camp. He was two years older than I and had started school for the first time that year a month earlier, in October. He took me to the main office and translated into Spanish some of the questions the principal asked me. Before I was led to my third-grade class, Miguelito and I agreed to meet on the playground after school and walk home together.

Miguelito was already waiting for me when I got to the playground. We started walking toward the labor camp, following the same route we had taken that morning. The path was muddy and full of puddles, just like the school playground. Miguelito and I imagined the puddles were lakes and we pretended to be giants stepping over them. We counted out loud the number of lakes we stepped over, trying to outdo each other. Miguelito had longer legs than I did, but I kept up with him until I slipped and lost my balance. My right foot landed right in one of the puddles, splashing muddy water on my clean overalls and on Miguelito. The cardboard inside my shoe got soggy and started to fall apart. Once I collected myself, Miguelito and I began laughing. We continued walking, but every time we looked at each other, we would start laughing again. This went on until we arrived at the labor camp.

As we approached our cabin, I knew no one was home because our *Carcachita*, our old jalopy, was not parked in front. "Want to come in?" I asked.

"I have to go home first," he answered. "I'll come back in a little while."

"I'll be in the back by the creek," I said. "Don't forget, our cabin is number ten."

"I live ten cabins down from you, number twenty," Miguelito replied cheerfully.

I went inside our cabin. It was cold and quiet. I went over to our window to look at our neighbor's goldfish. I watched it swim back and forth. *I wonder if he gets lonely,* I thought to myself. I then went out behind our cabin, and sat on a rock by the edge of the creek. I listened to the water murmur and watched the little gray fish play with each other. The current gently tugged at the plants grow-ing in the water. I picked up some pebbles and tossed them in one at a time, trying not to hit the fish.

"What are you doing?" asked Miguelito, coming up behind me and making me jump.

"I am just watching the little fish while I wait for my parents to get back from work."

"Do you want to catch some?"

"Catch what?" I asked.

"Fish, *tonto*," he replied, chuckling.

Before I could answer, he jumped up like a grasshopper, ran over to a small pepper tree that was a few yards away, and yanked off two branches. "These are our fishing poles," he said excitedly, handing one over to me. "Tomorrow I'll bring the other stuff and we'll finish making them."

That night it poured again, and in the morning the rain turned to drizzle. I put my hat on and walked out the door, hoping to meet Miguelito so we could walk to school together. I could not wait to catch fish with him in the afternoon, but he did not show up, and I did not see him at school all day. When I returned home from school that afternoon, I went to see if he was waiting for me by the creek. He was not there either. Then I remembered his cabin number. I hurried to number twenty and knocked on the door. No one answered. I went around to the side of the cabin and peeked through the window. The cabin was completely empty. My heart sank into my stomach. Slowly I walked home, feeling a lump in my throat. I heard Miguelito's laugh in my head and thought about our game with the puddles. When I got home I stood by our window and stared at our neighbor's goldfish for the longest time.

Finally my family arrived. They had spent all day driving around looking for work.

It rained so much that night that the creek flooded into the dirt streets, making the cabins look like they floated on a lake. Then, days later, when the clouds disappeared and the sun emerged, the lake began to split into hundreds of small puddles throughout the labor camp.

One day, on my way home from school, I discovered little gray fish in the puddles. I had no idea how they got there, but I noticed that in the smaller puddles the fish were dying. The mud was suffocating them. As I gazed at the dead fish, the image of the goldfish flashed in my mind. I quickly ran to our cabin and got the empty Hills Brothers coffee can. I filled it with water and began picking up the dying fish from the mud puddles, putting them in the can, and dumping them in the creek. After a couple of hours, I was exhausted. There were too many and I could not work fast enough to save them all. I prayed for rain, but the sun kept beating down, turning the puddles into mud.

I picked up one last, small dying fish and took it to our next-door neighbor who owned the goldfish. I knocked and knocked on the door until my hand hurt. No one was home. I placed the coffee can on the front steps and peered inside. The little gray fish looked up at me, rapidly opening and closing its mouth.

That evening I looked through the window into our

neighbor's cabin. The goldfish swam peacefully, alongside the little gray fish. I sighed and smiled to myself. The next morning I took the fishing rod Miguelito had given me, placed it gently in the creek, and watched it float away.

Christmas Gift

A few days before Christmas, Papá decided to move from the cotton labor camp in Corcoran and look for work elsewhere. We were one of the last families to leave because Papá felt obligated to stay until the rancher's cotton had been all picked, even though other farmers had better crops. Papá thought it was the right thing to do; after all, the rancher had let us live in his cabin free while we worked for him.

I did not mind too much moving for the third time that year. It rained most of the time we were there, and Papá, Mamá, and Roberto went days without work. Sometimes, in the evenings, we went into town in our *Carcachita* to look for food in the trash behind grocery stores. We picked up fruits and vegetables that had been thrown away because they were partly spoiled. Mamá sliced off the rotten parts and made soup with the good vegetable pieces, mixing them with bones she bought at the butcher shop. She made up a story and told the butcher the bones were for the dog. The butcher must have known the bones were for us and not a dog because he left more and more pieces of meat on the bones each time Mamá went back.

As we were packing to leave Corcoran that December, a young couple came to our door. Papá invited them in. The man, in his early twenties, wore a blue, faded shirt and khaki pants. His wife, about the same age as he, was dressed in a simple brown cotton dress and a gray wool sweater worn at the elbows and buttoned in the front. Taking off his cap, the man said apologetically, "We're sorry to bother you, but you know, with all this rain, and my wife expecting...well, we thought...perhaps you could help us out a little bit." He reached into a paper bag he was carrying and pulled out a small wallet. "Perhaps you could give us fifty cents for this? Look, it's pure leather; almost brand new," he said, handing it to Papá.

Shaking his head, Papá replied sympathetically, "I am sorry. I wish I could, *paisano*, but we're broke too."

When I heard Papá say "we're broke too," I panicked. My hope for getting a ball of my own that Christmas faded—but only for a second. "It can't be like last year," I told myself.

My thoughts were interrupted by the man's desperate insistence. "Please, how about twenty-five cents?" Before Papá could answer, the man quickly pulled out from the bag a white embroidered handkerchief, saying, "How about ten cents for this handkerchief? Please. My wife did the needlework on it."

"I am very sorry," Papá repeated.

"It's beautiful," Mamá said, gently placing her hand on the woman's fragile shoulder. "*Que Dios los bendiga*," she added.

Papá walked the couple out the door and accompanied them partway to the next cabin, where they continued trying to peddle their few possessions.

After we finished packing and loading our belongings in our *Carcachita*, Papá closed the door to the cabin and we headed north.

We were leaving only three weeks after I had enrolled in the fourth grade for the first time that year. As we drove by the school, I saw some kids I knew on the playground. I imagined myself playing with them with the ball I would get for Christmas. I waved to them but they did not see me.

After stopping at several places and asking for work, we found a rancher who still had a few cotton fields to be picked. He offered us work and a tent to live in. It was one of many dark green tents lined up in rows. The labor camp looked like an army settlement.

We unloaded the *Carcachita*, placed some cardboard on the dirt floor, and laid our wide mattress on it. All of us — Papá, Mamá, Roberto, Trampita, Torito, and Rubén, my baby brother — slept on the mattress to keep warm, especially during chilly nights when the freezing wind pierced the canvas walls of our new home.

As Christmas drew closer, the more anxious and excited I became. When December 24 finally arrived, time seemed to stand still. *One more day to wait,* I thought.

That evening, after supper, we all sat on the side of the mattress and listened to Mamá tell us the story about the birth of Jesus and the Three Wise Men who brought Him gifts. I only half listened. I wanted the evening to end quickly and for morning to come. Finally, sleep overcame my brothers and we turned in for the night. We huddled together and covered ourselves with army blankets we had bought at a secondhand store. I could not sleep thinking about Christmas. Once in a while, Papá's words "but we're broke too" entered my mind, but I pushed them out with fantasies of playing with my very own ball.

Thinking we were all asleep, Mamá quietly slipped out of bed and lit the kerosene lamp. I covered my head with the blanket, and through a hole in it I watched her, trying to see what gifts she was going to wrap. But she sat behind some wooden crates that served as the table and blocked my view. I could see only her weatherworn face. The shadow cast by the dim light made the circles under her eyes look even darker. As she began to wrap the gifts, silent tears ran down her cheeks. I did not know why.

At dawn, my brothers and I scrambled to get the presents that had been placed next to our shoes. I picked mine up and nervously tore at the butcher-paper wrapping: a bag of candy. Roberto, Trampita, and Torito looked sadly at me and at each other. They, too, had received a bag of candy. Searching for words to tell Mamá how I felt, I looked up at her. Her eyes were full of tears. Papá, who was sitting next to her on the mattress, lifted its corner and pulled out from underneath the white embroidered handkerchief. He tenderly handed it to Mamá, saying, *"Feliz Navidad, vieja."*

Death Forgiven

El Perico, my close friend, had a tragic ending. He was a red, green, and yellow parrot that had been smuggled from Mexico by Don Pancho, an undocumented farm worker who was my father's friend.

When we first got *El Perico*, he spent most of the time in a makeshift wire cage Roberto, my older brother, built for him. But once he learned to trust us and he became a family member, *El Perico* wandered around freely in the dilapidated garage where we lived while harvesting Mr. Jacobson's vineyards. Whenever he was out of the cage, we closed the garage door, the only opening large enough for him to fly out.

I, and the rest of my family, grew to love *El Perico*. I spent hours teaching him how to say "*periquito bonito*." His favorite pastime was walking back and forth across a thin, long wire that my mother sometimes used for hanging our clothes to dry. It stretched from one end of the garage to the other. I would place a grape box directly underneath *El Perico*, climb on it, stretch out my arm, and hold my index finger close to his toes so that he could perch on it. He would slowly walk sideways, tilting his head from side to side, repeating "*periquito bonito, periquito bonito*" as he grabbed my finger. I would lift him and bring him close to my face, touching my nose to his beak. He would stare at me sideways and rub his beak against my nose until I would kiss his head.

The affection *El Perico* and I had for each other was matched only by his attachment to Catarina, a spotted black cat that belonged to Chico and his wife, Pilar, a young Mexican couple who, like the parrot, were undocumented. They lived in one of the stables next to our garage. Chico, Pilar, and Catarina visited us often in the evenings after work. *El Perico* and Catarina grew on each other little by little. Eventually, they became such good friends that they even ate leftovers—beans, rice, and potatoes—from the same plate. When Chico and Pilar visited without Catarina, *El Perico* would get very upset. He would flap his wings and make such a loud, shrieking sound that it made the wire vibrate. This would irritate my father, who could not stand any noise, especially when he was tired from work, which was most of the time.

One early evening, Chico and Pilar came by themselves,

without Catarina. *El Perico* immediately threw a tantrum and began shrieking, louder than ever. The noise struck my father like lightning. He had been in a terrible mood the last few days because he was not sure where we would work, now that the grape season was almost over. Covering his ears with his hands, he bolted to the corner of the garage, grabbed the broom, and swung with all his might at my friend, who was perched on the wire. Red, green, and yellow feathers scattered everywhere. *El Perico* hit the dirt floor like a wet rag. Instantly Roberto, Mamá, and I started wailing. My father shouted at all of us to stop. Seeing a stream of blood dribble from *El Perico*'s silent beak, I felt as though someone had ripped my heart out. I threw the garage door open and darted out, running as fast as I could toward a storage shed that was about half a mile away. The shouting, screaming, and crying from our home chased me. I wanted to escape, to die. I finally reached the shed, dragged myself in, and closed the door behind me. It was dark and quiet. I fell to my knees and prayed and prayed for *El Perico*. The repetition of "*Santa María, Madre de Dios, ruega Señora por nosotros los pecadores ahora y en la hora de nuestra muerte, amén*" slowly comforted and soothed my soul. Then I prayed for my father.

The next day after work, Roberto, Trampita, and I buried *El Perico* in a cigar box we found in Mr. Jacobson's garbage can. We dug a hole about a foot deep in one of the rows in the vineyard behind the garage, placed the box inside, and covered it with dirt. Roberto made a small cross from sticks and laid it on the mound. We stood there silently for several minutes and then went home.

I visited his grave every day until we moved to Corcoran two weeks later to find work picking cotton.

Cotton Sack

In the latter part of October, after the grape season was over, we left Mr. Jacobson's vineyards in Fresno and headed for Corcoran to pick cotton. As we drove down the narrow, two-lane road, we passed vineyard after vineyard. Stripped of their grapes, the vines were now draped in yellow, orange, and brown leaves. Within a couple of hours the vineyards gave way to cotton fields. On both sides of the road we were surrounded by miles and miles of cotton plants. I knew that we were approaching Corcoran.

After stopping at three different cotton labor camps, we found one that gave us work and a one-room cabin to live in. It was one of several farm-worker dwellings lined up in a row.

That evening, after supper, Papá unfolded the sacks for picking cotton and laid them out in the middle of the floor to prepare them. I was surprised when I saw only three.

I knew the twelve-foot-long one was Papá's, and that the ten-foot-long ones were Mamá's and Roberto's. "Where is mine?" I asked. "Don't I get one?"

"You are still too little to have your own," Papá answered.

"But last year I picked without a sack," I replied, trying to hold back my tears.

Papá shook his head without saying another word. I knew from his silence that I should not insist on it.

Papá asked me to stretch out the middle of his sack while he sewed an extra piece of canvas onto the bottom to reinforce it. After finishing the last stitch, he tried it. He tied the sack around his waist, leaving the front opening between his thighs. Dragging the sack on the floor behind him, Papá stooped over, moving his hands up and down and around imaginary plants, pretending he was picking cotton. He looked like a kangaroo.

When he finished sewing Mamá's sack, she tried it just like Papá. When she saw the ten-foot white canvas trailing on the floor behind her, she burst out laughing.

"What's so funny?" asked Papá.

"This is the prettiest wedding dress I have ever seen," she answered, holding her stomach to ease the pain from laughing so much. Giggling, Roberto and I looked at Papá, who was not amused.

As usual, when it was time for bed, Papá folded his cotton sack to use as a pillow. He placed it at the end of the wide mattress so he faced the wall, on which hung a small, faded picture of *la Virgen de Guadalupe*. He then poured himself a glass of water from a gallon bottle and placed it on the floor near the bed, along with his aspirins, Camel cigarettes, and an empty, red Folger's coffee can, which we all used during the night when it was too cold to go to the outhouse. Roberto, Trampita, Torito, and I knelt in front of the *Virgen de Guadalupe* and said our prayers silently. Mamá wrapped Rorra, my newborn sister, in a baby blanket, laid her gently in a crate next to the mattress, and kissed her good night. She and Papá then slipped into bed on one end of the mattress; Roberto, Trampita, Torito, Rubén, and I crawled in on the other end. We snuggled against each other to keep warm. My parents had an advantage over the five of us because our legs did not reach the other end of the mattress. Their feet, however, did reach our end of the mattress, and sometimes I would wake up facing Mamá's and Papá's toes.

The pounding of the rain on the roof woke me several times during the night. Every time I opened my eyes, I saw the burning tip of Papá's cigarette glowing in the dark; other times I heard the rattle of his aspirin bottle. I did not mind the rain because it meant I could sleep in the next morning. The cotton would be too wet to pick. Because we got paid three cents a pound, most ranchers did not let us pick cotton when it was wet.

I woke up late. The rain had stopped and everyone except Rorra was already up. Papá, whose eyes were puffy and red, cursed the rain. He and Roberto wrapped the one-gallon water bottle with burlap and sewed it tightly to keep the bottle from breaking. Trampita and I sat on a box and watched Mamá make flour tortillas.

She used a twelve-inch lead pipe to roll the dough on a flat piece of board atop the wooden boxes that served as our dining table. As she pressed and rolled the dough, she kept turning it until it was perfectly round and about a quarter of an inch thick. Mamá then cooked the tortilla on a *comal* on one of the two burners of our small kerosene stove. She usually cooked a pot of beans on the other burner.

After we ate the freshly cooked tortillas and beans for breakfast, I helped Roberto wash the dishes in the aluminum tub, which Mamá also used for bathing Torito, Rubén, and Rorra and for washing clothes. And while Mamá mended Papá's shirt, he drove in our *Carcachita* to the nearest gas station to fill the one-gallon bottle with drinking water and to get more kerosene for the stove. When Papá returned, he smoked another cigarette, took two aspirins, and went to bed. Trampita and I sat on the mattress and played guessing games and then listened to Roberto's ghost stories. Mamá told us to be very quiet because Papá was not feeling well. "Remember, he does not like noise," she said.

For the next few days it rained off and on. By Friday, when the sun finally came out, Papá's aspirin bottle was empty and a pile of cigarette butts covered the floor by his side of the bed.

Like an alarm clock, the honking of the horn woke me with a start on Saturday morning. It was the *contratista*, the labor contractor, who drove around in his beat-up red Ford truck, honking the horn to let us know that the cotton was dry and ready to pick. Leaning on the horn, and trying to avoid the potholes full of water, he drove up and down the muddy paths, slow as a snail, between rows and rows of perfectly aligned one-room cabins. After finishing the round, which took about twenty minutes, he started again just in case some had fallen back asleep or had not heard him the first time.

On days when I was not in school, the honking of the horn was for me like the final bell on the last day of school. It meant I had to go to work. But for Papá, who usually hated any kind of noise, this loud sound was a tonic. It perked him up.

By the time the *contratista* finished the second round, Mamá had made the lunches and Papá was warming up the *Carcachita*. We loaded the sacks, climbed in, and lined up the car behind the *contratista's* red pickup truck, waiting for him to lead us to the cotton field that was to be picked. Loaded with workers who did not own cars, the pickup sluggishly pulled out, followed by the caravan of old battered cars and trucks.

After driving for about five miles, the *contratista* pulled

over to the side of the road and motioned us to park behind him. He got out and pointed to the cotton field. It
stretched from the shoulder of the road as far as the eye
could see. Papá, Mamá, Roberto, and I got out of the car.
Trampita stayed behind to take care of Torito, Rubén, and
Rorra. We followed Papá, who walked over to the cotton
plants to get a closer look. The other pickers did the same.
Papá said it was a good crop.

The plants were about three feet tall, and partly hidden between their dry brown leaves were many cotton
bolls. A few smaller plants had yellow and red flowers and
green bulbs that looked like small avocados. Papá explained that the flowers would close and form hard green
bulbs, which, in turn, would open to become cotton bolls.
"But remember," he said firmly, "cotton bolls are like roses.
They are pretty but they can hurt you."

"Yes, I know; the shell is like a cat's claw," I answered,
remembering the numerous scratches I had gotten on my
hands and wrists the year before.

After feeling the cotton to make sure it was completely
dry, the *contratista* told us to start working. All the pickers, except me, had their own sacks and their own rows to
harvest. I went a few yards ahead of Mamá and picked cotton from her row and piled it on the ground. When she
reached the pile, she picked it up and put it in her sack. I
then moved over to Papá's row and did the same for him
so that he and Mamá could move up their rows evenly.

Roberto did not need my help. He was a faster picker than either Papá or Mamá. After picking for two long hours, Roberto helped Mamá make more room in her sack by lifting it upright and shaking it several times up and down, compacting the cotton to the bottom.

When Mamá's sack was too heavy to drag behind her, Roberto took it to the weigh station to be emptied. The station was at the end of the field, about a quarter of a mile ahead. With my help, he flipped the sack over his left shoulder and held it in place with his right hand. I walked behind him, lifting the back end to lighten the load. The front end grazed the sides of the furrow as we made our way to the station. He stopped to rest a few times, and to wipe the sweat from his brow with the red and blue handkerchief tied around his collar. As we approached the weigh station, the *contratista* there said to Roberto, "You are really strong for such a little guy. How old are you?"

"Fourteen, almost fifteen," answered Roberto proudly and out of breath.

"No fooling," replied the *contratista*, adjusting the scale that hung from a tripod about three feet in front of the cotton trailer. After weighing Mamá's sack, the *contratista* jotted in a notebook "ninety pounds" after our last name, which he asked Roberto to spell. Teasingly he asked me, "Where is your sack, *mocoso*?" I pretended not to hear him and quickly walked around to the side of the trailer, which was about the size of our cabin. Its frame was covered by chicken wire, and it had no roof. It looked like a large bird cage. I held the ladder steady for Roberto while he climbed it carrying the sack. When he got to the top, he carefully walked to the middle of a plank that was laid across the trailer and emptied the cotton sack. Papá carried his own sack to the weigh station, but Roberto emptied it because Papá had a bad back.

At the end of the day, the *contratista* checked his notebook and handed my father eighteen dollars. "Not bad, six hundred pounds," Papá said grinning. *We could have done better if I had my own sack,* I thought to myself.

By the middle of November the cotton fields had been picked. The *contratista* informed Papá that we could stay in the cabin, which was owned by the company who owned the fields, until the end of the second picking, or *la bola*, as it was called in Spanish. *La bola* was messy and dirty. It involved harvesting everything left on the plants after the first picking, including cotton bulbs, shells, and leaves. The pay was one and a half cents per pound. The *contratista* told Papá that we could pick cotton for other ranchers until *la bola* would start, which was in two or three weeks.

For the next few days, when it did not rain, Papá, Mamá, and Roberto left the cabin early in the morning to look for work. They took Torito, Rubén, and Rorra with them. Trampita and I went to school and joined them in the fields on weekends and holidays.

At dawn on Thanksgiving Day, Papá, Roberto, and I

drove in our *Carcachita* for miles, looking for cotton fields that were being picked. During that four-day weekend, I was determined to prove to Papá that I should get my own sack.

On both sides of the road we passed endless fields of harvested cotton plants. From their dry branches dangled cotton fibers left during the first picking. They were frozen from the cold. In the distance ahead of us, Papá spotted a white speck and a cloud of thick black smoke. "*Allá,*" he said cheerfully, pointing with his finger. He stepped on the gas. As we approached the cotton field, Papá slowed down and parked our sputtering *Carcachita* on the roadside, near the cotton trailer. A few feet from it, around a burning tire, stood several men and women trying to keep warm.

Papá asked the Mexican foreman for work. He told Papá we could start anytime we wanted, but he suggested waiting until it got warmer. He invited us to join the others around the fire. Papá did not want to waste time. He told Roberto and me we could wait, but he was going to pick. Seeing this as an opportunity to prove to Papá that I was grown-up enough for my own cotton sack, I followed him and Roberto into the field.

They each took a row. I went ahead about a quarter of the way into Papá's row. I took my hands out of my pockets and started picking and piling the cotton in the furrow. Within seconds my toes were numb and I could hardly move my fingers. My hands were turning red and purple.

I kept blowing on them, trying to keep warm. Then I felt the urge to relieve myself. I turned around to make sure no one was looking. The workers, warming themselves by the fire, were too far away to see me. I cupped my left hand and caught the warm, yellowish stream in it and rubbed my hands together. Instantly, I felt fire as the salt stung the scratches on my skin. Then as the liquid quickly cooled, my hands felt like ice. I could not go on. Frustrated and disappointed, I walked over to Papá. He straightened up and looked down at me. His eyes were red and watery from the cold. Before I said anything, he looked at Roberto, who bravely kept on picking, and told me to go over to the fire. I knew then I had not yet earned my own cotton sack.

The Circuit

It was that time of year again. Ito, the strawberry share-cropper, did not smile. It was natural. The peak of the strawberry season was over, and in the last few days the workers, most of them *braceros*, were not picking as many boxes as they had during June and July.

As the last days of August disappeared, so did the num-ber of *braceros*. Sunday, only one — the best picker — came to work. I liked him. Sometimes we talked during our half-hour lunch break. That is how I found out he was from Jalisco, the same state in Mexico my family was from. That Sunday was the last time I saw him.

When the sun had tired and sunk behind the mountains, Ito signaled us that it was time to go home. "*Ya esora,*" he yelled in his broken Spanish. Those were the words I wait-ed for twelve hours a day, every day, seven days a week,

week after week. And the thought of not hearing them again saddened me.

As we drove home Papá did not say a word. With both hands on the wheel, he stared at the dirt road. My older brother, Roberto, was also silent. He leaned his head back and closed his eyes. Once in a while he cleared from his throat the dust that blew in from outside.

Yes, it was that time of year. When I opened the front door to the shack, I stopped. Everything we owned was neatly packed in cardboard boxes. Suddenly I felt even more the weight of hours, days, weeks, and months of work. I sat down on a box. The thought of having to move to Fresno and knowing what was in store for me there brought tears to my eyes.

That night I could not sleep. I lay in bed thinking about how much I hated this move.

A little before five o'clock in the morning, Papá woke everyone up. A few minutes later, the yelling and screaming of my little brothers and sister, for whom the move was a great adventure, broke the silence of dawn. Soon after, the barking of the dogs accompanied them.

While we packed the breakfast dishes, Papá went outside to start the *Carcachita*. That was the name Papá gave his old black Plymouth. He had bought it in a used-car lot in Santa Rosa. Papá was very proud of his little jalopy. He had a right to be proud of it. He had spent a lot of time looking at other cars before buying this one. When he finally chose the *Carcachita,* he checked it thoroughly before driving it out of the car lot. He examined every inch of the car. He listened to the motor, tilting his head from side to side like a parrot, trying to detect any noises that spelled car trouble. After being satisfied with the looks and sounds of the car, Papá then insisted on knowing who the original owner was. He never did find out from the car salesman, but he bought the car anyway. Papá figured the original owner must have been an important man because behind the rear seat of the car he found a blue necktie.

Papá parked the car out in front and left the motor running. "*Listo,*" he yelled. Without saying a word Roberto and I began to carry the boxes out to the car. Roberto carried the two big boxes, and I carried the two smaller ones. Papá then threw the mattress on top of the car roof and tied it with ropes to the front and rear bumpers.

Everything was packed except Mamá's pot. It was an old large galvanized pot she had picked up at an army surplus store in Santa Maria. The pot had many dents and nicks, and the more dents and nicks it acquired the more Mamá liked it. "*Mi olla,*" she used to say proudly.

I held the front door open as Mamá carefully carried out her pot by both handles, making sure not to spill the cooked beans. When she got to the car, Papá reached out to help her with it. Roberto opened the rear car door, and Papá gently placed it on the floor behind the front seat. All of us then climbed in. Papá sighed, wiped the sweat from his forehead with his sleeve, and said wearily, "*Es todo*."

As we drove away, I felt a lump in my throat. I turned around and looked at our little shack for the last time.

At sunset we drove into a labor camp near Fresno. Since Papá did not speak English, Mamá asked the camp foreman if he needed any more workers. "We don't need no more," said the foreman, scratching his head. "Check with Sullivan down the road. Can't miss him. He lives in a big white house with a fence around it."

When we got there, Mamá walked up to the house. She went through a white gate, past a row of rosebushes, up the stairs to the house. She rang the doorbell. The porch light went on and a tall, husky man came out. They exchanged a few words. After the man went in, Mamá clasped her hands and hurried back to the car. "We have work! Mr. Sullivan said we can stay there the whole season," she said, gasping and pointing to an old garage near the stables.

The garage was worn out by the years. It had no windows. The walls, eaten by termites, strained to support the roof full of holes. The dirt floor, populated by earthworms, looked like a gray road map.

That night, by the light of a kerosene lamp, we unpacked and cleaned our new home. Roberto swept away the loose dirt, leaving the hard ground. Papá plugged the holes in the walls with old newspapers and tin can tops. Mamá fed my little brothers and sister. Papá and Roberto then brought in the mattress and placed it on the far corner of the garage. "Mamá, you and the little ones sleep on the mattress. Roberto, Panchito, and I will sleep outside under the trees," Papá said.

Early the next morning Mr. Sullivan showed us where his crop was, and after breakfast, Papá, Roberto, and I headed for the vineyard to pick.

Around nine o'clock the temperature had risen to almost one hundred degrees. I was completely soaked in sweat, and my mouth felt as if I had been chewing on a handkerchief. I walked over to the end of the row, picked up the jug of water we had brought, and began drinking. "Don't drink too much; you'll get sick," Roberto shouted. No sooner had he said that than I felt sick to my stomach. I dropped to my knees and let the jug roll off my hands. I remained motionless with my eyes glued on the hot sandy ground. All I could hear was the drone of insects. Slowly I began to recover. I poured water over my face and neck and watched the dirty water run down my arms to the ground.

I still felt dizzy when we took a break to eat lunch. It was past two o'clock; we sat underneath a large walnut tree that was on the side of the road. While we ate, Papá jotted down the number of boxes we had picked. Roberto drew designs on the ground with a stick. Suddenly I noticed Papá's face turn pale as he looked down the road. "Here comes the school bus," he whispered loudly in alarm. Instinctively, Roberto and I ran and hid in the vineyards.

We did not want to get in trouble for not going to school. The neatly dressed boys about my age got off. They carried books under their arms. After they crossed the street, the bus drove away. Roberto and I came out from hiding and joined Papá. "*Tienen que tener cuidado,*" he warned us.

After lunch we went back to work. The sun kept beating down. The buzzing insects, the wet sweat, and the hot dry dust made the afternoon seem to last forever. Finally the mountains around the valley reached out and swallowed the sun. Within an hour it was too dark to continue picking. The vines blanketed the grapes, making it difficult to see the bunches. "*Vámonos,*" said Papá, signaling to us that it was time to quit work. Papá then took out a pencil and began to figure out how much we had earned our first day. He wrote down numbers, crossed some out, wrote down some more. "*Quince,*" he murmured.

When we arrived home, we took a cold shower underneath a water hose. We then sat down to eat dinner around some wooden crates that served as a table. Mamá had cooked a special meal for us. We had rice and tortillas with *carne con chile,* my favorite dish.

The next morning I could hardly move. My body ached all over. I felt little control over my arms and legs. This feeling went on every morning for days until my muscles finally got used to the work.

It was Monday, the first week of November. The grape season was over and I could now go to school. I woke up early that morning and lay in bed, looking at the stars and savoring the thought of not going to work and of starting sixth grade for the first time that year. Since I could not sleep, I decided to get up and join Papá and Roberto at breakfast. I sat at the table across from Roberto, but I kept my head down. I did not want to look up and face him. I knew he was sad. He was not going to school today. He was not going tomorrow, or next week, or next month. He would not go until the cotton season was over, and that was sometime in February. I rubbed my hands together and watched the dry, acid-stained skin fall to the floor in little rolls.

When Papá and Roberto left for work, I felt relief. I walked to the top of a small grade next to the shack and watched the *Carcachita* disappear in the distance in a cloud of dust.

Two hours later, around eight o'clock, I stood by the side of the road waiting for school bus number twenty. When it arrived I climbed in. Everyone was busy either talking or yelling. I sat in an empty seat in the back.

When the bus stopped in front of the school, I felt very nervous. I looked out the bus window and saw boys and girls carrying books under their arms. I put my hands in my pant pockets and walked to the principal's office. When I entered I heard a woman's voice say, "May I help you?" I was startled. I had not heard English for months. For a few seconds I remained speechless. I looked at the lady, who waited for an answer. My first instinct was to answer her in Spanish, but I held back. Finally, after struggling for English words, I managed to tell her that I wanted to enroll in the sixth grade. After answering many questions, I was led to the classroom.

Mr. Lema, the sixth-grade teacher, greeted me and assigned me a desk. He then introduced me to the class. I was so nervous and scared at that moment when everyone's eyes were on me that I wished I were with Papá and Roberto picking cotton. After taking roll, Mr. Lema gave the class the assignment for the first hour. "The first thing we have to do this morning is finish reading the story we began yesterday," he said enthusiastically. He walked up to me, handed me an English book, and asked me to read. "We are on page 125," he said politely. When I heard this, I felt my blood rush to my head; I felt dizzy. "Would you like to read?" he asked hesitantly. I opened the book to page 125. My mouth was dry. My eyes began to water. I could not begin. "You can read later," Mr. Lema said understandingly.

During recess I went into the restroom and opened my English book to page 125. I began to read in a low voice, pretending I was in class. There were many words I did not know. I closed the book and headed back to the classroom.

Mr. Lema was sitting at his desk correcting papers. When I entered he looked up at me and smiled. I felt better. I walked up to him and asked if he could help me with the new words. "Gladly," he said.

The rest of the month I spent my lunch hours working on English with Mr. Lema, my best friend at school.

One Friday, during lunch hour, Mr. Lema asked me to take a walk with him to the music room. "Do you like music?" he asked me as we entered the building. "Yes, I like *corridos*," I answered. He then picked up a trumpet, blew on it, and handed it to me. The sound gave me goose bumps. I knew that sound. I had heard it in many *corridos*. "How would you like to learn how to play it?" he asked. He must have read my face because before I could answer, he added, "I'll teach you how to play it during our lunch hours."

That day I could hardly wait to tell Papá and Mamá the great news. As I got off the bus, my little brothers and sister ran up to meet me. They were yelling and screaming. I thought they were happy to see me, but when I opened the door to our shack, I saw that everything we owned was neatly packed in cardboard boxes.

Learning the Game

I was in a bad mood. It was the last day of seventh grade before summer vacation. I had known the day was coming, but I had tried not to think about it because it made me sad. For my classmates, it was a happy day. During the afternoon, Miss Logan asked for volunteers to share what they were going to do during the summer; lots of hands went up. Some talked about going away on trips; others about summer camp. I folded my hands under the desk, lowered my head, and tried not to listen. After a while, I managed to tune out what they were saying and only heard faint voices coming from different parts of the room.

In the school bus on the way home, I took out my note pad and pencil from my shirt pocket and began figuring out how much time there was before I would start school again—from the middle of June until the first week of November, about four and a half months. Ten weeks picking strawberries in Santa Maria and another eight weeks harvesting grapes and cotton in Fresno. As I added the number of days, I started to get a headache. Looking out the window, I said to myself, "One hundred thirty-two more days after tomorrow."

As soon as I arrived home, I took two of Papá's aspirins and lay down. I had just closed my eyes when I heard Carlos, our neighbor, shouting outside. "Come on, Panchito, we're starting the game."

The game was kick-the-can. I played it with Carlos and my younger bothers, Trampita, Torito, and Rubén, on school days when I had no homework, and on weekends when I was not too tired from working in the fields.

"Hurry, or else!" Carlos hollered impatiently.

I liked the game, but I did not enjoy playing with Carlos. He was older than I, and often reminded me of it, especially when I disagreed with him. If we wanted to play, we had to follow his rules. No one could play unless he said so. He wore tight jeans and a white T-shirt with the sleeves rolled up to show off his muscles. Under his right sleeve, he tucked a cigarette pack.

"Come on, Panchito!" Trampita yelled. "You're making us wait."

I went outside to play. I wanted to forget about the next 133 days.

"It's about time," Carlos said, giving me a light punch on the right shoulder. "You'll be the guard," he said, pointing at Rubén. "Trampita, you draw the circle. Torito, you get the can." As Carlos was giving orders, I saw Manuelito standing by one of the garbage cans. During every game, he stood by himself on the sidelines because Carlos would not let him play. "Let Manuelito be the guard," I said to Carlos.

"No way," he responded annoyingly. "I already told you before, he can't play. He's too slow."

"Come on, Carlos, let him play," I insisted.

"No!" he shouted, giving me and Manuelito a dirty look.

"Go ahead and play, Panchito," Manuelito said timidly. "I'll stand here and watch."

We started the game, and the more we played, the less I thought about my troubles. Even my headache went away. We played until dark.

The alarm clock went off early the next morning. I glanced at the window. It was still dark outside. I shut my eyes, trying to get one more minute of sleep, but Roberto, my older brother, jumped out of bed and pulled off the covers. "Time to get up!" he said. When I saw him putting on his work clothes, I remembered we were going to work, and not to school. My shoulders felt heavy.

On the way to the fields, Papá turned on the *Carcachita*'s headlights to see through the thick fog that blew in from the coast. It covered the valley every morning, like a large, gray sheet. Ito, the sharecropper, was waiting for us when we arrived. Then a black pickup truck appeared. We could see it through the wall of fog, not far from where we parked. The driver stopped behind our *Carcachita* and, in perfect Spanish, ordered the passenger who rode in the bed of the truck to get off.

"Who's that?" I asked Papá, pointing to the driver.

"Don't point," Papá said. "It's bad manners. He's Mr. Díaz, the *contratista*. He runs the *bracero* camp for Sheehey Berry Farms. The man with him is one of the *braceros*."

In his broken Spanish, Ito introduced us to Gabriel, the man who accompanied the *contratista*.

Gabriel looked a few years older than Roberto. He wore a pair of loose, tan pants and a blue shirt. The shirt was faded. His straw hat was slightly tilted to the right, and he had long, dark sideburns that were trimmed and came down to the middle of his square jaw. His face was weather-beaten. The deep cracks in the back of his heels were as black as the soles of his *guaraches*.

Gabriel took off his hat and we shook hands. He seemed nervous. But he relaxed when we greeted him in Spanish.

After the *contratista* left, we marched in line to the end of the field, selected a row, and started to work. Gabriel ended up between Papá and me. Because it was Gabriel's first time harvesting strawberries, Ito asked Papá to show him how to pick. "It's easy, Don Gabriel," Papá said. "The main thing is to make sure the strawberry is ripe and not bruised or rotten. And when you get tired from squatting, you can pick on your knees." Gabriel learned quickly by watching and following Papá.

At noon, Papá invited Gabriel to join us for lunch in our *Carcachita*. He sat next to me in the back seat while Roberto and Papá sat in the front. From his brown paper bag, he pulled out a Coke and three sandwiches: one of mayonnaise and two of jelly. "Not again! We get this same lunch from that Díaz every day," he complained. "I am really tired of this."

"You can have one of my *taquitos*," I said.

"Only if you take this jelly sandwich," he responded, handing it to me. I looked at Papá's face. When I saw him smile, I took it and thanked him.

"Do you have a family, Don Gabriel?" Papá asked.

"Yes, and I miss them a lot," he answered. "Especially my three kids."

"How old are they?" Papá asked.

"The oldest is five, the middle one is three, and the little one, a girl, is two."

"And you, Don Pancho, how many do you have?"

"A handful," Papá answered, grinning. "Five boys and a girl. All living at home."

"You're lucky. You get to see them every day," Gabriel said. "I haven't seen mine for months." He continued as though thinking out loud. "I didn't want to leave them, but I had no choice. We have to eat, you know. I send them a few dollars every month for food and things. I'd like to send them more, but after I pay Díaz for room and board and transportation, little is left." Then, in an angry tone of voice, he added, "Díaz is a crook. He overcharges for everything. That *sin vergüenza* doesn't know who he's dealing with."

At this point, we heard the honking of a car horn. It was Ito signaling us that it was time to go back to work. Our half-hour lunch break was over.

That evening, and for several days after, I was too tired to play outside when we got home from work. I went straight to bed after supper. But as I got more and more used to picking strawberries, I began to play kick-the-can again. The game was always the same. We played by Carlos's rules and he refused to let Manuelito play.

Work was always the same, too. We picked from six o'clock in the morning until six in the afternoon. Even though the days were long, I looked forward to seeing Gabriel and having lunch with him every day. I enjoyed listening to him tell stories and talk about Mexico. He was as proud of being from the state of Morelos as my father was about being from Jalisco.

One Sunday, near the end of the strawberry season, Ito sent me to work for a sharecropper who was sick and need-ed extra help that day. His field was next to Ito's. Gabriel was loaned out to the same farmer. As soon as I arrived, the *contratista* began giving me orders. "Listen, *huerquito*, I want you to hoe weeds. But first, give me and Gabriel a hand," he said. Gabriel and I climbed onto the bed of the truck and helped him unload a plow. The *contratista* tied one end of a thick rope to it and, handing the other end to Gabriel, said, "Here, tie this around your waist. I want you to till the furrows."

"I can't do that," Gabriel said with a painful look in his face.

"What do you mean you can't?" responded the *contratista*, placing his hands on his hips.

"In my country, oxen pull plows, not men," Gabriel replied, tilting his hat back. "I am not an animal."

The *contratista* walked up to Gabriel and yelled in his face, "Well this isn't your country, idiot! You either do what I say or I'll have you fired!"

"Don't do that, please," Gabriel said. "I have a family to feed."

"I don't give a damn about your family!" the *contratista* replied, grabbing Gabriel by the shirt collar and pushing him. Gabriel lost his balance and fell backward. As he hit the ground, the *contratista* kicked him in the side with the tip of his boot. Gabriel sprung up and, with both hands clenched, lunged at the *contratista*. White as a ghost, Díaz quickly jumped back. "Don't be stupid . . . your family," he stammered. Gabriel held back. His face was flushed with rage. Without taking his eyes off Gabriel, the *contratista* slid into his truck and sped off, leaving us in a cloud of dust.

I felt scared. I had not seen men fight before. My mouth felt dry and my hands and legs began to shake. Gabriel threw his hat on the ground and said angrily, "That Díaz is a coward. He thinks he's a big man because he runs the *bracero* camp for the growers. He's nothing but a leech! And now he tries to treat me like an animal. I've had it." Then, picking up his hat and putting it on, he added, "He can cheat me out of my money. He can fire me. But he can't force me to do what isn't right. He can't take away my dignity. That he can't do!"

All day, while Gabriel and I hoed weeds, I kept thinking about what happened that morning. It made me angry and sad. Gabriel cursed as he hacked at the weeds.

When I got home from work that evening, I felt restless. I went outside to play kick-the-can. "Come on guys, let's play!" Carlos yelled out, resting his right foot on the can.

I went up to Manuelito, who was sitting on the ground and leaning against one of the garbage cans. "You heard Carlos, let's play," I said loudly so that Carlos could hear me.

"He didn't mean me," Manuelito answered, slowly getting up.

"Yes, you too," I insisted.

"Is it true, Carlos?" Manuelito asked.

"No way!" Carlos shouted.

Manuelito put his hands in his pockets and walked away.

"If Manuelito doesn't play, I won't either," I said. As soon as I said it, my heart started pounding. My knees felt weak. Carlos came right up to me. He had fire in his eyes. "Manuelito doesn't play!" he yelled.

He stuck his right foot behind my feet and pushed me. I fell flat on my back. My brothers rushed over to help me up. "You can push me around, but you can't force me to play!" I yelled back, dusting off my clothes and walking away. Trampita, Torito, Rubén, and Manuelito followed me to the front of our barrack.

Carlos stood alone inside the circle in the dirt, looking at the can and glancing at us once in a while. After a few moments, he cocked his head back, spat on the ground, and swaggered toward us, saying, "OK, Manuelito can play."

Screaming with joy, Manuelito and my brothers jumped up and down like grasshoppers. I felt like celebrating, too, but I held back. I did not want Carlos to see how happy I was.

The following morning, when Ito told us that the *contratista* had gotten Gabriel fired and sent back to Mexico, I felt like someone had kicked me in the stomach. I could not concentrate on work. At times I found myself not moving at all. By the time I had picked one crate, Papá had picked two. He finished his row, started a second, and caught up to me.

"What's the matter, Panchito?" he asked. "You're moving too slow. You need to speed it up."

"I keep thinking about Gabriel," I answered.

"What Díaz did was wrong, and someday he'll pay for

it, if not in this life, in the next one," he said. "Gabriel did what he had to do."

Papá pushed me along, handing me several handfuls of strawberries he picked from my row. With his help, I got through that long day.

When we got home from work, I did not want to play kick-the-can. I wanted to be alone, but my brothers would not let me. They followed me around, asking me to play.

I finally gave in when Manuelito came over and joined them. "Please, just one game," he pleaded.

"OK, just one," I answered.

We drew sticks to see who would play guard. Carlos was it. While he counted to twenty with his eyes closed, we ran and hid. I went behind a pepper tree that was next to the outhouse. When Carlos spotted me, he shouted, "I spy Panchito!" We both raced to the can. I got to it first and kicked it with all my might. It went up in the air and landed in one of the garbage cans. That was the last time I played the game.

To Have and to Hold

As usual, after the strawberry season was over in Santa Maria, Papá decided to move to the San Joaquin Valley in Central California to pick grapes. Like the year before, we had spent the summer months picking strawberries for Ito, the Japanese sharecropper. This time, however, we were not going to Fresno to harvest Mr. Sullivan's vineyards. Papá did not want us to live in Mr. Sullivan's old garage again. So we headed for Orosi, a small town a few miles southeast of Fresno. Papá had heard that a grape grower there, named Mr. Patrini, had nice places for farm workers to live.

We packed our belongings and left Santa Maria in September, the week school started. Papá drove. Mamá and Roberto sat in the front seat. My younger brothers, Trampita, Torito, and Rubén, and I sat in the back. Rorra, my little sister, slept on Mamá's lap. Everyone was quiet. The only noise came from passing cars and the droning of the *Carcachita*'s motor. As we passed by Main Street School, I reached underneath the front seat and pulled out my penny collection, which I kept in a small, white cardboard box. I then felt my shirt pocket for my blue note pad. I took it out, placed it on the box, and held them both tightly in my hands as I stared out the window, wondering what Orosi would be like.

After we had been traveling for a few miles, I put my note pad back in my shirt pocket, took the top off my coin box, and starting looking at my pennies. I divided them into two layers separated by cotton. On top were my two favorites: a 1910 Lincoln Head and an 1865 Indian Head.

The 1910 Lincoln Head penny had belonged to Papá, but he gave it to me. We were living in Delano, and every day after coming home from picking grapes, Papá took out his small metal box where he kept our savings and placed the day's earnings inside. One Sunday evening, when he emptied the box on the table to count the money, a penny rolled off and landed next to me. I picked it up and handed it to him.

"Do you know how old this coin is?" he asked.

"No," I said.

"It was made in 1910, the year I was born," he said proudly.

"It's a very old penny!" Mamá said, chuckling as she cooked supper on our kerosene stove.

Papá glanced over at Mamá, laughed, and replied, "It's only a couple of years older than you, *vieja*." Holding it in his hand, Papá continued, "The Revolution started that same year."

"What revolution?" I asked.

"The Mexican Revolution," he responded. "I don't know the whole story," he said apologetically. "I didn't go to school, but what I do know I learned from listening to *corridos* and to your *abuelita* Estefanía. She told me that during that time, many of the rich *hacendados* treated the *campesinos* like slaves."

"Did *abuelito* Hilario fight in the Revolution?" I asked.

"No, *mi'jo*. My father died six months after I was born. But your *abuelita* favored the Revolution, just like all poor people did. I also heard that many *hacendados* buried their money and jewels in the ground to hide them from the revolutionaries. Many of those treasures have never been found. But they say that yellowish red flames shoot out from underneath the ground where the treasure is buried, and that you can see the blazes from far away at night." Then with a twinkle in his eyes, he added, "I don't know if that's true, but that's what they say."

Papá reached out, took my right hand, and placed the penny in it, saying, "You can have it. This way you'll never forget the year I was born. And, if you keep on saving pennies, someday you'll have your own treasure."

I was so excited I almost forgot to thank Papá. I examined the penny closely. The year 1910 was worn.

That is when I started collecting pennies. I liked the older ones best.

As we made our way up the San Luis Obispo grade, I placed the Lincoln Head penny back in the box and took out my 1865 Indian Head coin.

Carl had given it to me when I was in the fifth grade in Corcoran. He and I were good friends in school. And when we found out that we both collected coins, we became the best of friends. We made sure we got on each other's team when we played ball during recess, and we ate our lunch together every day.

One Friday after school, Carl invited me to his home to see his coin collection. As soon as the last bell rang, we ran to his house, which was only three blocks away. When I walked in, I was amazed. I had never been inside a house before. The rug under my feet felt like a sack full of cotton. The living room was warm and as big as the one-room cabin we lived in. The light was soft and soothing. Carl then showed me his room. He had his own bed and his own desk. From the closet, which was half full of clothes, he pulled out a cigar box and several dark blue folders.

"These are my pennies," he said, opening one of the

folders. His coins were all neatly organized by year. My eyes and fingers went straight to the oldest. "That's an 1860 Indian Head," he said.

"I thought all pennies were Lincoln Heads," I said in surprise.

"Oh, no!" he exclaimed, opening his cigar box. "See, I have lots of them."

"I'll give you one of my Lincoln pennies for one of your Indian Heads," I said.

Carl thought about it for a while and then said, "You don't have to. I'll give you one. Pick the one you want."

"Thanks," I said excitedly. I quickly went through the loose pennies in his box and picked one made in 1865. It was the oldest one I could find.

On the way back to school to catch my bus, Carl said, "When can I come to your house and see your collection?" His question took me by surprise. I never thought he would want to visit me at our home. And after seeing his house, I was not sure I wanted him to see where I lived. "Well... when?" he asked again, looking a bit confused because I did not answer him.

After thinking of possible excuses, I finally said, "I live too far. I'll bring my collection to school. It's not much, just a few Lincoln Head pennies."

"That's okay, I'd like to see it anyway," he said.

I never got the chance to show Carl my collection.

That weekend we moved to Five Points, and I never saw my friend again.

I placed the penny back in the box and closed it. I looked straight ahead through the windshield, between Papá and Mamá, to see how far we had traveled, and to look for road signs to Orosi.

"What does *Orosi* mean?" I asked Papá.

"I am not sure, *mi'jo*," he responded. "But I have a feeling we're going to like it there."

I took out my note pad and wrote the word down, breaking it into two syllables. Oro-si. *Oro* meant "gold" in Spanish, and *si* meant either "yes" or "if." Based on what Papá said, I figured it meant "yes" in this case.

I closed the note pad and held it in the palm of my hand. It was almost brand new when I found it in the city dump in Santa Maria. Now its blue soft covers were beginning to fade and its corners were frayed. As I smoothed them out with my fingers, I recalled when I first started to use it.

I was in Miss Martin's sixth-grade class in Santa Maria. It was the end of January, and we had just returned from Fresno where I had started the sixth grade in Mr. Lema's class in November. I was behind in English, Miss Martin's favorite subject. Every day she would write a different English word on the blackboard and ask the class to look it up in our dictionaries as fast as we could. The student who found the word the quickest would get a point, and, at the end of the week, the one with the most points would get a gold star. I never got a star or a point. It took me too long to find the words, and I did not know what many of them meant. So I got the idea of writing the words down in my note pad, along with their definitions, and memorizing them. I did this for the rest of the year. And after I left Miss Martin's class, I continued adding new words and their definitions to my note pad. I also wrote other things I needed to learn for school and things I wanted to know by heart, like spelling words, and math and grammar rules. I carried the note pad in my shirt pocket and, while I worked in the fields, memorized the information I had written in it. I took my *librito* with me wherever I went.

After traveling for about five hours, we arrived at our new home in Orosi. It was an old, two-story, yellow wooden house. It was located about fifteen miles outside the city limits. Mr. Patrini, the owner, told us that the house was seventy years old. We could not use the second level because the floors were unstable. The first floor had two rooms and a kitchen. Behind the house was a large barn and hundreds of vineyards.

It did not take long to unload our *Carcachita* and settle in. Papá, Mamá, and Rorra took one room; Roberto, Trampita, Torito, Rubén, and I moved into the other one. After my brothers and I had put away our few things, I sat on the floor and looked at my pennies. I wanted to make sure they were not rubbing against each other in the box before placing them underneath the mattress. When I looked up, Rorra was standing next to me.

"Can I have one?"

"One what?" I asked.

"A penny," she answered.

"Not one of these," I said. "These are special." She made a face and walked away stomping her tiny feet.

That evening, before going to bed, I checked on my pennies again. I then took off my shirt and carefully hung it on a nail in the wall and made sure my note pad did not fall out the pocket. After our prayers, we slipped into bed. I had trouble falling asleep. *I can't believe we are living in a house,* I thought to myself.

My little brothers must have been excited too because they started whispering and giggling. Roberto tried to quiet them down, but they would not stop. "Listen," Roberto said in a loud whisper. "I hear *La Llorona* weeping upstairs."

"I don't hear anything. You're just trying to scare us," Trampita answered.

"No, I am not," Roberto responded. "Just be quiet and you'll hear her." There was dead silence for the rest of the night.

The next day, before sunrise, Papá, Roberto, Trampita, and I went to pick grapes for Mr. Patrini. Mamá stayed home to take care of my little sister and brothers. I took my note pad with me. I wanted to learn some spelling rules while I worked, but I couldn't. The angry, blistering sun did not let me. By ten o'clock my shirt was soaking wet. I wiped my hands on my pants and carefully removed the note pad from my shirt pocket and took it to the *Carcachita* and left it there. I did not want it to get dirty and wet. By the end of the day, my whole body was covered with dust from the vineyards. My arms and hands looked like they were made of clay. I scraped the muddy layer off them with the hooked knife I used for cutting grapes.

At sundown, when we got home, Mamá and Rorra drove to the store while Papá, Roberto, Trampita, and I stripped to our underwear and bathed in a trough that was behind the house. After we got dressed, I placed the note pad in the pocket of my clean shirt.

When Mamá returned, I helped her with the groceries. "Did you get any pennies in change?" I asked.

She looked in her purse and handed me one. It was made in 1939. "Can I have it?"

"Of course, *mi'jito*," she answered.

I went to our room to add it to my collection. I took out my coin box from underneath the mattress and removed the top. The first layer of white cotton was bare. *No, they have to be here*, I thought to myself. I swiftly removed the cotton and checked the second layer. Nothing. My 1910 and 1865 pennies were gone! I rushed out of the room, shouting, "My pennies! Someone took them!"

When I got to the kitchen, Rorra ran and hid behind

Mamá, who was standing by the stove preparing dinner. "Did you take my pennies?" I yelled at my sister. "If you did, give them to me!"

Holding on to Mamá's leg with her left arm, Rorra extended her right hand and offered me two red gumballs. "I don't want your gum, I want my two pennies," I shouted. She dropped the gumballs and started whimpering.

"Calm down, Panchito," Mamá said. Then looking down at my sister, she said, "*Mi'ja*, did you take Panchito's pennies?" Rorra nodded sheepishly. "And what did you do with them?" Mamá continued. Rorra pointed to the gumballs on the floor. "Did you put the pennies in the gum machine at the store?" she asked.

When my sister nodded again, my heart dropped to my stomach. I felt my face on fire. Everything blurred. I stormed out of the house, slammed the door behind me, sat on the front stairs, and cried.

Seconds later, Mamá came out and sat beside me. "I know how disappointed you are, *mi'jito*, but your sister is only four years old," she said tenderly. Then clearing her throat, she continued. "Let me tell you a story I heard when I was a little girl. Long ago there lived a very smart ant who saved her pennies for so many years that she became rich. Many animals wanted to marry her, but they frightened her. The cat mewed too much, the parrot talked too much, and the dog barked too loud. A bull and a goat also scared her, but not a little brown mouse named *El Ratoncito*.

He was quiet, intelligent, polite, and mannerly. They got married and lived happily for a very long time. But one day, when the ant was cooking a pot of beans, she fell in it and drowned, leaving *El Ratoncito* with a lot of pennies, but terribly sad and lonely. So you see, *mi'jito*, Rorra is more important than the pennies. Don't be so hard on your little sister."

Mamá's story calmed me down a little, but I was still angry at Rorra. I took a deep breath and went back inside to our room. I sat on the mattress and pulled out my note pad from my shirt pocket. I turned to the page where I listed my pennies, and crossed out Lincoln Head, 1910, and Indian Head, 1865.

The following morning, before going to work, Mamá and I covered my note pad with waxed paper to keep it clean. I then marked the spelling rules I wanted to memorize that day. As I picked grapes, I went over them in my mind, looking at my notes only when I had to. This made the time go by faster.

On our way home from work, we stopped at a gas station to get kerosene for our stove. The attendant filled our five-gallon tank and placed it in the trunk of the *Carcachita*. When we arrived home, Papá gave Roberto the car keys and asked us to unload the tank and refill the stove with it.

"Panchito, this does not smell like kerosene," Roberto said as he took out the tank from the trunk. "It smells like gasoline. You'd better go tell Papá."

I went inside and told Papá. He was nailing a wall board that had come loose in our room. "I am sure it's fine, *mi'jo*. It's probably cheap kerosene," he answered as he continued hammering.

I took off my shirt, placed it on the mattress, and then went back outside. "Papá said it's okay," I told Roberto.

He shrugged his shoulders, picked up the tank, and carried it to the kitchen. Mamá was getting ready to cook dinner. She cleared the stove to make it easier for Roberto to refill it. The stove sat on a small table underneath a window that had plastic curtains. When Roberto was finished, Mamá placed the pot of beans on one of the burners. She then lit a match. As soon as she touched it to the burner, the stove burst into flames, setting the curtains on fire.

"¡Ay, *Dios mío!*" Mamá exclaimed, pushing Roberto and me away from the stove. "*Viejo*, the kitchen is on fire," she yelled. I was terrified. The plastic curtains curled up. Pieces of melted plastic fell to the floor, giving off dark smoke that smelled like burned rubber. Roberto picked up the dishpan full of soapy water and hurled it over the stove. It made the fire worse. Like thirsty tongues, the flames chased the water as it ran and spread on the floor.

"Get out," Papá shouted as he rushed in the kitchen and saw the flames. "Out, out!" he repeated. Mamá, Roberto, and I ran to the front of the house. Trampita, Rubén, Rorra, and Torito were already outside. We all stood by the *Carcachita*. When I saw Mamá sobbing, I felt more scared.

A few moments later Papá came out coughing and clenching in his arms something wrapped in a blanket. His hair was singed. He placed the bundle on the ground and uncovered it.

The instant I saw the silver metal box, I thought of my note pad. "*¡Mi librito!*" I screamed out, recalling that I had left it in my shirt on the mattress.

I dashed toward the house, but Roberto quickly caught up to me and grabbed me by the back of the T-shirt and yelled, "Are you crazy?"

"I have to save it!" I cried out, pulling away from him.

Papá hurried over and stood in front of me. "*¡Ya! ¡No seas tonto*, Pancho!" he shouted angrily. His glare frightened me. I stopped struggling to get away. Roberto let go of me. I clenched my fists and tried to hold back my tears.

By the time the firemen came, the house had burned down completely. The dying flames looked like they were coming from under the ground.

Papá picked up our savings box, started walking toward the barn, and said wearily, "Let's stay in the barn tonight. Tomorrow we'll look for another place."

Everyone followed him except me. I stayed behind.

"Come on, Panchito," Mamá said.

When she saw I was not moving, she came up to me and placed her arm around me. I burst out crying. Lifting my chin with her right hand and looking me straight in the eyes, Mamá said, "We're safe and we have each other, *gracias a Dios*."

"Yes, but what about my *librito*. It's gone, just like my pennies," I responded.

After a long pause she said, "Do you know what was in your *librito?*"

"Yes," I answered, wondering why she asked.

"Well . . . if you *know* what was in your *librito*, then it's not all lost."

I heard Mamá's words but did not understand what she meant until a few days later. We had moved to a labor camp also owned by Mr. Patrini and were picking grapes again. It was a scorching, hot day. My clothes were drenched in sweat. I crouched underneath the vines for shade, but the heat pierced right through. I recalled the fire and placed my right hand over my shirt pocket. It was empty. Feeling a lump in my throat, I started thinking about Carl, my pennies, the house. Then, for a long time, I thought about my *librito* and what Mamá said. I could see in my mind every word, every number, every rule, I had written in my note pad. I knew everything in it by heart. Mamá was right. It was not all lost.

Moving Still

For days, when I got home from school, I found Papá lying flat and complaining about not being able to pick cotton because his back was killing him. He often talked about leaving Corcoran and going back to Santa Maria, but he kept changing his mind, hoping to get better. He constantly worried that we would not have enough money saved at the end of the cotton season to carry us over the winter months. It was already the end of December, and Roberto, my older brother, was the only one working. Mamá stayed home to take care of Papá, Rorra, and Rubén. My other two younger brothers, Torito and Trampita, went to school with me, and on weekends, when it did not rain, we went to work with Roberto. The only cotton left for us to harvest was *la bola*, the leftovers from the first picking, which paid one and a half cents a pound.

But one day when I got home, Papá did not complain

about anything, not even his back. As soon as I entered the cabin, he strained to straighten up from the mattress that lay on the floor and exclaimed, "*Mi'jo,* are you all right?"

"*Sí,* Papá," I responded, wondering why he looked so worried.

"*Gracias a Dios,*" he said. "*La migra* swept through the camp about an hour ago, and I didn't know if the immigration officers searched your school too."

Mamá must have noticed the fright in my eyes when I heard the word "*migra*" because she immediately came and hugged me.

That word evoked fear ever since the immigration raid in Tent City, a labor camp in Santa Maria where we sometimes lived. It was a Saturday, late afternoon. I was playing marbles with Trampita in front of our tent when I heard someone holler, "*¡La migra! ¡La migra!*" I looked over my shoulder and saw several vans screech to a halt, blocking the entrance to the camp. The vans' doors flew open. Out dashed armed men dressed in green uniforms. They invaded the camp, moving through tents, searching for undocumented workers who ran into the wilderness behind the camp, trying to escape. Many, like Doña María, *la curandera,* were caught, herded, and hauled away in the Border Patrol vehicles. A few managed to get away. We were lucky. Mamá and Roberto had gone to town to buy groceries. Papá showed the officers his "green card" that Ito had helped him get, and they did not ask about Trampita or me.

When Roberto came home from work that evening, Papá and Mamá were relieved to see him. "You didn't see *la migra?*" Papá asked.

"It came to our camp but missed us," Mamá said, rubbing her hands together.

"It didn't come to the field," Roberto responded.

"So you didn't go out with *la migra*," Papá said jokingly, trying to ease the tension.

Roberto went along with Papá's joke. "No, Papá, she's not my type," he answered. We all laughed nervously.

When Papá stopped laughing and bit his lower lip, I knew what was coming. "You have to be careful," he warned us, waving his index finger at Roberto and me. "You can't tell a soul you were born in Mexico. You can't trust anyone, not even your best friends. If they know, they can turn you in." I had heard those words so many times, I had memorized them. "Now, where were you born, Panchito?" he asked in a firm tone, giving me a piercing look.

"Colton, California," I answered.

"Good, *mi'jo*," he said.

Roberto then handed Papá the money he had earned that day. Papá clenched his fists, looked away toward the wall, and said, "I am useless; I can't work; I can't feed my family; I can't even protect you from *la migra*."

"Don't say that, Papá," Roberto answered. "You know that's not so."

Papá glanced at Roberto, lowered his eyes, and asked

me to bring him the small, silver metal box where he kept our savings. When I brought it, he sat up slightly, opened it, and counted the money inside. "If I work in Santa Maria, we might be able get through this winter with what we've saved," he said worriedly. "But what if my back won't let me?"

"Don't worry, Papá," Roberto responded. "Panchito and I can find work in Santa Maria thinning lettuce and topping carrots."

Seeing this as a chance to persuade my father to leave Corcoran, and knowing I was anxious to return to Santa Maria, Mamá winked at me and said to Papá, "Roberto is right, *viejo*. Let's leave. Besides, the immigration may come around again. It's safer living in Santa Maria."

After a long pause, Papá finally said, "You're right. We'll go back to Bonetti Ranch, tomorrow morning."

Like swallows returning to Capistrano, we would return to our nest, Bonetti Ranch in Santa Maria, every year after the cotton season was over in Corcoran. The ranch became our temporary home. We had lived there in barracks eight months out of the year, from January through August, ever since Tent City, the farm labor camp, had been torn down. The ranch was located on East Main Street but had no address. Most of the residents were Mexican field laborers who were American citizens or had immigrant visas like Papá. This made the ranch relatively safe from Border Patrol raids.

I was so excited about going back to Bonetti Ranch that I was the first one up the following morning. After we packed our belongings and loaded them into the car, we headed south to Santa Maria. I could hardly contain myself. Roberto and Trampita were excited too. I imagined this was how kids felt when they talked about going away on vacation. Papá could not drive because of his back pain, so Roberto drove. The trip took about five hours, but it seemed like five days to me. Sitting in the back seat, I opened the window and stuck my head out, looking for road signs saying SANTA MARIA. "Can't you go faster?" I asked impatiently, poking Roberto in the back.

"Sure, if you want us to get a ticket," he responded.

"That's all we need," Papá said, chuckling. "If that happens, we may just as well turn ourselves in to *la migra*."

I immediately closed the window and sat back without saying a word.

After traveling for a couple of hours, Mamá suggested we stop to have lunch, which she had prepared that morning. I was hungry, but I did not want to waste time. "We can eat in the car," I said, hoping my little sister and brothers would go along with my idea.

"What about Roberto? He can't eat and drive," Papá responded.

We stopped by the side of the road to eat. Papá slowly got out of the car, holding on to Roberto's arm and mine. He lay on the ground and stretched his back. I gobbled my two-egg-and-chorizo tacos and, making sure Papá was not looking, signaled to Roberto to hurry. "*Ya pues*, Panchito," he said, a bit annoyed. "I am almost finished."

After lunch we continued our trip. The closer we got to Santa Maria, the more excited I became because I knew where we were going to live for the next several months. I especially looked forward to seeing some of my classmates in the eighth grade at El Camino Junior High. I had not seen them since last June when school ended. *I wonder if they'll remember me?* I thought to myself.

As we drove by Nipomo, the last town before Santa Maria, my heart started pounding. And as soon as I saw the Santa Maria bridge, which marked the entrance to the city limits, I yelled out, "We're here! We're here!" Trampita and Torito also began to cheer and woke up Rubén, who had fallen asleep. Mamá looked at us and laughed.

"*Se han vuelto locos*," Papá said, smiling and gesturing with his hand that we had gone crazy.

Once we crossed the cement bridge, which went over a dry riverbed for a quarter of a mile, I stretched my neck and tried to pinpoint the location of Bonetti Ranch. I knew it was near where Tent City used to be, about a mile south of the city dump.

The highway became Broadway and went right through the center of the town. When we got to Main Street, Roberto turned left and drove east for about ten miles. Along the way, I kept pointing out places I recognized:

Main Street School; Kress, the five-and-dime store; the
Texaco gas station where we got our drinking water; and
the hospital where Torito stayed when he got sick. We
then crossed Suey Road, which marked the end of the
city limits and the beginning of hundreds of acres of re-
cently planted lettuce and carrots.

When we turned into Bonetti Ranch, I noticed nothing had changed from the year before. We were greeted
by dozens of stray dogs. Roberto had to slow down the
Carcachita to a crawl to avoid hitting them, and to dodge
the deep potholes in the dirt path that circled the front of
the barracks. A few of the dogs belonged to the residents,
but most of them had no owners. They slept underneath
the dwellings and ate whatever they found in the garbage.
But they were never alone. They were plagued by hundreds
of bloodthirsty fleas. I felt sorry for them and wondered if
they were bothered by the fleas as much as I was when they
invaded our bed at night.

The barracks were still the same. Mr. Bonetti, the owner, continued to ignore them. Looking like victims of a war,
the dwellings had broken windows, parts of walls missing,
and large holes in the roofs. Scattered throughout the ranch
were old, rusty pieces of farm machinery. In the middle of
the ranch was a large storehouse where Mr. Bonetti kept
lumber, boxes of nails, and other building supplies that he
planned to use someday.

We rented and moved into the same barrack we had lived in the previous year. We covered the gaps between wallboards with paper, painted the inside, and covered the kitchen floor using paint and pieces of linoleum we found at the city dump. We had electricity. And even though we could not drink the water because it was oily and smelled like sulphur, we used it for bathing. We heated it in a pot on the stove and poured it into the large aluminum container that we used for a bathtub. To get drinking water, we took our five-gallon bottle and filled it at the Texaco gas station downtown. Along the front edge of our barrack, Roberto planted red, pink, and white geraniums. Around them, he built a fence and painted it, also using supplies from the city dump.

To the right of our house, a few yards away, stood three large empty oil barrels that served as garbage cans for the residents. Mr. Bonetti periodically burned the garbage and hauled the remains to the city dump in his truck. Behind our barrack was the outhouse that we shared with two other families. Sometimes, on rainy days, the earth underneath would shift and tilt the toilet to one side, making it difficult to balance inside. Mr. Bonetti nailed a rope to the side wall inside to give us something to hold on to.

The week after we arrived in Santa Maria, we enrolled in school. Roberto started the tenth grade at Santa Maria High School for the first time that year; Trampita and

Torito resumed elementary school at Main Street School. At El Camino Junior High I continued the eighth grade, which I had started in Corcoran the first week of November, after the grape season was over. Rubén and Rorra were still too young for school. Mamá stayed home to take care of them.

Even though this was my first time in the eighth grade at El Camino, I did not feel too nervous. I remembered a few of the kids in my class because they had been in my seventh-grade class the year before. Some I hardly recognized. They had grown taller, especially the boys. I had stayed the same, four feet eleven inches. I was one of the smallest kids in the school.

I liked my two teachers. I had Mr. Milo for math and science in the mornings and Miss Ehlis for English, history, and social studies in the afternoons. In history, we concentrated on the U.S. government and the Constitution. I enjoyed Mr. Milo's class the most because I did better in math than in English. Every Thursday Mr. Milo gave us a math quiz, and the following day he arranged our desks according to how well we did on the test. The student with the highest score had the honor of sitting in the front seat, first row. Sharon Ito, the daughter of the Japanese sharecropper for whom we picked strawberries during the summer, and I alternated taking the first seat, although she sat in it more often than I did. I was glad we did not have the same seating arrangement for English!

As days went by, Papá's back did not get better, and neither did his mood. Mamá, Roberto, and I took turns massaging him with Vicks VapoRub. When he was not complaining about not being able to work, he lay in bed, motionless, with an empty look in his eyes. He took a lot of aspirins, ate very little, and hardly slept during the night. During the day, when he was exhausted, he took short naps.

Early one evening, when Papá had dozed off, Mamá took Roberto and me aside. "I don't think your Papá can work in the fields anymore," she said, rubbing her hands on her apron. "What are we going to do?"

After a long pause, Roberto answered, "I've been thinking about getting a job in town. I am tired of working in the fields."

"Yes, a job that is year-round," Mamá said.

"That's a good idea!" I said enthusiastically. "Then we won't have to move to Fresno again."

"Maybe Mr. Sims can help me," Roberto said.

"Who's Mr. Sims?" Mamá asked.

"He's the principal of Main Street School," I answered. "Remember? He gave me a green jacket."

Trying to help her memory, Roberto added, "He also bought me a pair of shoes when he saw mine were worn out. I was in the sixth grade."

"Ah, sí. Es muy buena gente," Mamá said, finally recalling who he was.

Mr. Sims agreed to help Roberto find a part-time job in

town. He told my brother he would let him know when he found something. Meanwhile, Roberto and I continued working, thinning lettuce and topping carrots, after school and on Saturdays and Sundays.

Several days later, Mr. Sims told Roberto that he had found a job for him. He set up an appointment for my brother to see the owner of the Buster Brown Shoe Store on Broadway that Saturday afternoon. Roberto, Mamá, and I were very excited.

Early Saturday morning, Roberto and I headed for work thinning lettuce. As he drove, Roberto could not stop talking about his new job at the shoe store. His appointment that afternoon seemed a long time away. To make the hours in the field go by faster, we decided to challenge ourselves. We marked a spot in our rows, about a third of the way in, to see if we could reach it without straightening up. "Ready? Go!" Roberto said.

I stooped over and began thinning with my six-inch hoe. After about twenty minutes without rest I could no longer stand the pain in my back. I dropped to my knees and continued thinning without stopping. As soon as I reached the marked spot, I fell over. Roberto did too. "We did it," I said out of breath. "But my back is killing me." To ease the pain, I lay flat on my stomach in the furrow and Roberto pressed down on my back with his hands. I felt relief as my spine cracked.

"You're getting old, Panchito. Let's rest," Roberto said, laughing. I chuckled between moans.

Roberto lay on his stomach next to me. I turned over on my back and looked up at the gray sky. The dark clouds threatened rain.

"I am tired of moving every year," Roberto said, picking up small dirt clods and tossing them.

"Me too," I said. Then, following a moving cloud with my eyes, I asked, "Do you ever wonder what we'll be doing ten or twenty years from now? Or where we'll be living?"

Looking around to make sure no one was listening, Roberto whispered, "If we don't get deported..." Then he added confidently, "In Santa Maria, of course. I can't imagine living anywhere else. What about you?"

Recalling the different labor camps we lived in, I answered, "I don't want to live in Selma, Visalia, Bakersfield, or Corcoran." After thinking about it for a while, I said, "I like Santa Maria. So if you decide to live here forever, I will too."

Right after lunch, Roberto left work to clean up and keep his appointment. I continued working and thinking about Roberto's new job. Every few minutes I straightened up to give my back a rest. "This is our chance to stay in Santa Maria all year and not move to Fresno to pick grapes and miss school," I said to myself. The more I thought about the idea, the more excited I became. *Perhaps Roberto will get me a job at the shoe store too,* I thought. "How about that, Buster Brown!" I said out loud, flipping the hoe in the air and catching it by the handle. Just as I finished my row, it started to rain. I ran for cover under a pepper tree and waited for Roberto.

When he returned to pick me up, his mood was darker than the sky. "What's the matter?" I asked. "You didn't get the job?"

Roberto shook his head. "No, I got the job," he said. "But not working at the store."

"Doing what then?" I asked impatiently.

"Cutting his lawn. Once a week," Roberto answered sadly. His lips quivered.

"Oh, no!" I exclaimed, throwing my hoe on the ground in anger.

Roberto cleared his throat, wiped his eyes with his shirt-sleeve, and said, "I am going to see Mr. Sims after school on Monday. Maybe he can suggest something else." He picked up my hoe and handed it to me. "Don't lose faith, Panchito," he said, putting his arm around me. "Things will work out."

Monday morning, my mind was not on school. I kept worrying about Papá and thinking about Roberto. *I hope he gets a job,* I thought. "But what if he doesn't? No, he will," I said to myself.

To make things worse, that afternoon Miss Ehlis gave our class an assignment I was not expecting. "I am passing out an important part of the Declaration of Independence that I want you to memorize," she said, counting the number of sheets to hand out in each row. Her announcement evoked a series of moans and groans from the class. "Now, there is no need for that," she said smiling. "The part I want you to know by heart is very short." Once everyone had the sheet of paper, she read the first few lines to the class.

"'We hold these truths to be self-evident: that all men are created equal; that they are endowed by their creator with certain inalienable rights; that among these are life, liberty, and the pursuit of happiness; that to secure these rights, governments are instituted among men, deriving their just powers from the consent of the governed.' You see, it's not difficult. You can recite it to me independently or, for extra credit, in front of the class."

We were to let her know our preference the following week. For me there was only one choice: to recite it to her privately. I did not want to get in front of the class and risk being laughed at because of my Mexican pronunciation. I knew I had a thick accent, not because I heard it myself, but because kids sometimes made fun of me when I spoke English. I could not take a chance of this happening in front of the whole class, even though I wanted to get the extra credit.

That afternoon after school, I took the bus home. On the way, I tried to memorize the lines of the Declaration of Independence, but I had trouble concentrating. I kept wondering what Mr. Sims told Roberto. When I got home and saw the *Carcachita*, I knew Roberto was already there. I rushed in. Papá, Mamá, and Roberto were sitting at the kitchen table. "What happened? Tell me!" I said excitedly.

"What do you think?" Roberto asked, trying to conceal his smile.

I glanced at Papá and Mamá. They were beaming. "You got a job!" I cried out.

"Yes. Mr. Sims offered me the janitorial job at Main Street School," he answered, grinning from ear to ear.

"It's a year-round job," Mamá said, looking at Papá.

Being careful with his back, Papá stood up slowly and hugged her gently. He then turned to Roberto and said, "Education pays off, *mi'jo*. I am proud of you. Too bad your Mamá and I didn't have the opportunity to go to school."

"But you've taught us a lot, Papá," I answered. I had not seen Papá that happy for weeks.

After supper, I sat at the table to do my homework. I was so excited about Roberto's new job that it was difficult to focus. But I was determined to memorize the lines from the Declaration of Independence and recite them perfectly, without forgetting a single word. I took the text and broke it down, line by line. I looked up in the dictionary the words I did not know: *self-evident, endowed, inalienable*, and *pursuit*. I added them to the list of English words I kept in my new, black pocket note pad. I had gotten in the habit of writing down a different English word and its definition every day and memorizing it. After I looked up the meaning of the words, I wrote the entire text in my note pad in tiny letters: "We hold these truths to be self-evident: that all men are created equal." I went over the first line many times until I memorized it. My plan was to memorize at least one line a day so that I could recite it on Friday of the following week.

On Wednesday after school, Roberto drove to El Camino Junior High to pick me up so that I could help him clean Main Street School. It was starting to rain. When we arrived at the school, we headed down to the basement to the janitor's room to get the cleaning cart. It held a large cloth trash bag, a dust broom, a sponge, and toilet supplies. As we entered the first classroom we were to clean, it brought back memories. It was the same room I had been in in the first grade, when I had Miss Scalapino. Everything looked the same except that the desks and chairs seemed a lot smaller. I sat down at the teacher's desk, took out my pocket note pad, and read the second and third lines I needed to memorize: "that they are endowed by their creator with certain inalienable rights; that among these are life, liberty, and the pursuit of happiness." I went over to the cart, picked up the wet sponge, and began wiping the blackboard as I recited the lines in my head. Thunder and lightning interrupted my concentration. I looked out the window. It was pouring rain. Through the reflection on the windowpane, I could see Roberto behind me dust-mopping the floor.

By Friday, I had memorized the introductory lines to the Declaration of Independence and could recite them with relative ease. Only the word *inalienable* caused me problems. I had trouble saying it, so I broke it into syllables and repeated each sound slowly, followed by the whole word. On my way to school on the bus, I took out the black note pad from my shirt pocket, closed my eyes, and practiced saying "in-a-li-en-a-ble" silently to myself. The kid sitting next to me gave me a puzzled look and asked, "Are you trying to say something?"

His question took me by surprise. "No," I answered. "Why do you ask?"

"Well, you keep moving your lips."

A bit embarrassed, I told him what I was doing. I don't think he believed me because he stared at the note pad I was holding in my hand, mumbled, and changed seats.

The school day started out just right. In the morning, Mr. Milo returned the math exams to the class and asked us to rearrange our seats according to our scores. I sat in the first seat in the first row. This was definitely a good sign. I even looked forward to my recitation in Miss Ehlis's class that afternoon.

At one o'clock, right after lunch, I was the first one in Miss Ehlis's classroom. I sat at my desk and went over the recitation in my mind one last time: "We hold these truths to be self-evident: that all men are created equal; that they are endowed by their creator with certain inalienable rights; that among these are life, liberty, and the pursuit of happiness." I checked the text in my note pad to make sure I had not forgotten anything. It was perfect. Feeling confident, I placed the note pad inside the desk and waited for the class to start.

After the bell rang and everyone was seated, Miss Ehlis began to take roll. She was interrupted by a knock at the door. When she opened it, I could see Mr. Denevi, the principal, and a man standing behind him. The instant I saw the green uniform, I panicked. I wanted to run, but my legs would not move. I began to tremble and could feel my heart pounding against my chest as though it wanted to escape too. Miss Ehlis and the immigration officer walked up to me. Putting her right hand on my shoulder, and looking up at the officer, she said sadly, "This is him." My eyes clouded. I stood up and followed the immigration officer out of the classroom and into his car marked "Border Patrol." I sat in the front seat as the officer drove down Broadway to Santa Maria High School to pick up Roberto.

A Note from the Author

The stories in *The Circuit*, like other stories I have written, are semiautobiographical. They are based on my childhood experiences of growing up in a family of migrant farm workers. The inspiration for writing them comes from my teachers and the community of my childhood.

When I started school, I did not know a word of English; I knew only Spanish. In fact, I failed my first year of school because I did not know English well enough. I had no self-confidence in English until I met Mr. Lema, a wonderful sixth-grade teacher whom I describe in the collection's title story, "The Circuit." I enrolled in his class after having missed the first two months of school because I was helping my family pick grapes and cotton. I was far behind other children in class but, thanks to Mr. Lema, I made good progress. During the lunch hour, he gave me extra help.

Although I did not speak English well and Mr. Lema did

not speak Spanish, we managed to communicate with each other. He valued my Mexican cultural background and my native language while he taught me English. At times it was frustrating for both of us, but he never lost his patience with me. He never made me feel inadequate or inferior because of my poor English-language skills.

Miss Bell, my sophomore English teacher, was also very influential. From her I learned to appreciate literature and the art of writing. She regularly assigned our class to write narrative accounts of personal experiences. Even though I had difficulty expressing myself, I enjoyed writing about my migrant childhood. In one of my essays, she commented that the experiences I wrote about were very moving and that my writing showed promise. She then had me read *The Grapes of Wrath*. It was difficult for me, but I could not put it down. It was one of the first literary works to which I could relate. The more I read it, the more I appreciated the value and power of language to move hearts and minds.

After graduating from Santa Maria High School, I received several scholarships to attend Santa Clara University, where I discovered that my migrant experiences were both an obstacle and a blessing. They were an obstacle to the extent that I did not have the privileged social, economic, and educational experiences most of my classmates enjoyed. However, they were a blessing because they served as a constant reminder of how fortunate I was to be in college. Those experiences convinced me that I should do everything within my power to forge ahead in my studies and not give up. I compare my situation then to a man who is drowning. A man who is drowning uses the water, the very substance that threatens his life, to save himself. So I used poverty and those experiences that initially pulled me down to boost myself up. Whenever I felt discouraged, I would write about my childhood.

Upon graduating from Santa Clara University, I received a graduate fellowship to Columbia University in New York, where I met Andrés Iduarte, a Mexican professor and writer who became my thesis advisor. Following his advice to publish my work, I gathered the notes I had taken over the years and wrote "*Cajas de cartón*" (Cardboard Boxes), which was published in a New York Spanish-language literary magazine. Translated into English under the title "The Circuit," it was published in the *Arizona Quarterly* and received the Arizona Quarterly Annual Award for best story.

For the next several years, I continued my efforts to write more short stories, but teaching and administrative responsibilities left me little time for writing. Then I applied for and received a sabbatical for 1995. I devoted the entire year to researching and writing *The Circuit*.

In writing these stories, I relied heavily on my childhood recollections, but I also did a lot of background research. I interviewed my mother; my older brother, Roberto; and other relatives. I looked through photographs and family documents, and I listened to *corridos*, Mexican ballads, that I had heard as a child. I also went to different places in the San Joaquin Valley where we had lived in migrant labor camps: Bakersfield, Fowler, Selma, Corcoran, Five Points. I visited museums in those towns and read through newspapers from that era. Unfortunately, I found little or no information or documentation in those sources about migrant farm workers. I was disappointed, but it convinced me even more that I should write this book. As I gathered material, I began to recall other experiences I had forgotten with the passage of time. Looking back at those childhood memories from an adult point of view, I made a series of discoveries about myself in relation to my family, my community, and our society. I gained a deeper sense of purpose and meaning as an educator and as a writer.

My greatest challenge was to write about my childhood experiences from the point of view of the child and to make them accessible to both children and adults. I wanted readers to hear the child's voice, to see through his eyes, and to feel through his heart.

Why did I write these stories? I wrote them to chronicle part of my family's history but, more importantly, to voice the experiences of a large sector of our society that has been frequently ignored. Through my writing I hope to give readers an insight into the lives of migrant farm workers and their children whose back-breaking labor of picking fruits and vegetables puts food on our tables. Their courage and struggles, hopes and dreams for a better life for their children and their children's children give meaning to the term "American dream." Their story *is* the American story.

—F.J.

From Francisco Jiménez's acceptance speech for the Boston Globe–Horn Book Award for Fiction, 1998